"I approached Judith Landau's new book with curiosity, unsure of what I might find. What I discovered was a work of striking clarity and emotional intelligence that bridges clinical insight with the mysteries of human experience. Her exploration of past-life regression is grounded, precise, and extremely compelling. This book challenged my assumptions and left me reconsidering what I thought I understood about memory and healing."

Patrick Griswold, MSN, MEd, RN, LAC, *Professor, Department of Human Services and Counseling, Metropolitan State University of Denver, USA*

"Most of my life, I have been a person who wants to understand. I want to analyze the data, weigh the evidence, and finally decide with certainty what is right or wrong, real or unreal, possible or impossible. Yet, as I have grown, both within the clinical world of behavioral health and as a human being, I have come to a humbling realization. Many of our most important truths are not found under a microscope but are discovered in places shrouded in mystery.

In this work, Judith invites us into that shroud and reveals how the echoes of the past, whether literal memories or powerful metaphors, shape our present-day suffering and our capacity for joy. From the 'Place of Joy' method to the exploration of ancestral shadows, she demonstrates how deep healing can occur when we look beyond the immediate symptoms and permit ourselves to consider a broader expanse of human experience.

For my fellow helping professionals, this book is both instructional and powerfully inspiring. For me, to harvest the wisdom found in these pages, I found I had to be willing to read from a place of embracing mystery. We often treat 'mystery' as a problem to be solved, but Judith treats it as a sanctuary where healing happens. She reminds us that 'what looks like madness may be memory', and that the soul has its own logic that the conscious mind cannot always measure.

Whether you view these accounts as literal reincarnation, the collective unconscious, or the soul's way of using metaphor to survive, the result is the same: transformation. I highly recommend this work to anyone who has ever felt that 'the missing piece' of healing, growth, or clinical care might just be found in the parts of the human experience we cannot yet explain."

D. John Dyben, DHSc, MCAP, CMHP, MFT, *Chief Clinical Officer, Hanley Foundation, USA*

"Dr. Landau brings life and light to the unexplainable phenomena of past life regression. She writes lyrically and explicitly highlights her real-life experiences with her patients and research. Dr. Landau provides us with her foundation of belief, trust and compassionate care. It's a fascinating read!"

Mel Pohl, MD, FASAM, *Chief Medical Officer, The Pointe Malibu Recovery Center, USA*

"Throughout her remarkable career, Dr. Judith Landau has consistently reminded us that suffering never exists in isolation. Long before systemic and relational models became more widely embraced, she has explored beyond purely biological explanations to understand individuals within their family systems, cultural contexts, and intergenerational legacies.

In *Intergenerational Healing Through Past Life Regression Family Hypnotherapy*, Landau and Sparcino expand that vision even further. With decades of clinical experience and wisdom, they explore past life regression hypnotherapy as an additional dimension through which families may understand and transform inherited patterns and work towards collective healing."

Constant Mouton, MD, *Psychiatrist, the Netherlands*

"In the intimacy of these deeply personal stories, heart, mind and soul open to voices of suffering and healing. Landau and Sparcino transport even the most skeptical reader to witness the reality of the soul manifesting beyond the limits of a single lifetime. Whether seeking relief from suffering, hoping to find more effective clinical strategies, or curious about the practical use of ancient wisdom for healing, the reader is transported as the text opens the boundary between mind and spirit. We witness the power of remembering as the soul reaches across time, generations, even species to locate and heal deep wounds. One who suffers is held in compassionate awareness by skilled healers whose work builds 'a bridge between science and spirit.' Judith Landau is widely recognized as a psychiatrist, family therapist, and sage therapist for networks and communities. She has been a shamanic healer since childhood. Her inclusion of Charlene Sparcino as co-author clearly demonstrates her commitment to relationship as fundamental to healing."

David Trimble, PhD, *Psychologist, Center for Multicultural Training in Psychology, USA*

Intergenerational Healing Through Past Life Regression Family Hypnotherapy

This book provides a compelling introduction to Past Life Regression Hypnotherapy.

Blending clinical insight, narratives of client experiences, and shamanic wisdom, the book explores memory, trauma, spiritual awakening, and healing. Through vivid metaphors, therapeutic frameworks, and soul-centered practices, it illuminates how healing becomes possible when we learn to witness ourselves and have others witness us with compassion and curiosity.

Intergenerational Healing Through Past Life Regression Family Hypnotherapy is an ideal resource for both individual and family therapists, counselors, and general clinicians looking to integrate past life regression hypnotherapy into their practice. It will also appeal to anyone interested in past lives.

Judith Lessing Landau is a child and family neuropsychiatrist and a former professor of psychiatry and family medicine. She specializes in facilitating healing and recovery through family therapy and Past Life Regression Hypnotherapy around the world.

Charlene Connie Sparcino is a mental health counselor, hypnotherapist, and spiritual practitioner integrating past life regression, clinical training, and shamanic study to guide clients toward clarity, healing, and awakened spiritual purpose.

Intergenerational Healing Through Past Life Regression Family Hypnotherapy

Judith Lessing Landau and
Charlene Connie Sparcino

Routledge
Taylor & Francis Group
NEW YORK AND LONDON

Designed cover image: Getty Images © SimoneN

First published 2027
by Routledge
605 Third Avenue, New York, NY 10158

and by Routledge
4 Park Square, Milton Park, Abingdon, Oxon, OX14 4RN

Routledge is an imprint of the Taylor & Francis Group, an informa business

ISBN: 978-1-041-06591-3 (hbk)
ISBN: 978-1-041-06590-6 (pbk)
ISBN: 978-1-003-63618-2 (ebk)

DOI: 10.4324/9781003636182

Typeset in Sabon
by SPi Technologies India Pvt Ltd (Straive)

To Pamela, my wife, best friend, and partner of many lifetimes, who gives meaning to this book
And to all our children and grandchildren, who give me hope for the future
And to all the patients who so graciously permitted us to share their personal stories
And to my co-author, Charlene Sparcino, who showed me that writing can be fun

– JLL

For my mother, whose tenderness taught me how to listen beneath the surface of things and whose love shaped the foundation of my life.
To my family, who continue to remind me what healing looks like in real time.

And to Dr. Judith Landau, whose invitation into this project became a threshold, one that reshaped my path and deepened my calling. I am grateful for your friendship, trust, and wisdom.

– CCS

Contents

About the Authors

Judith Lessing Landau, MD, DPM, LMFT, CFLE, CIP, CAI, is a child, family, and community neuropsychiatrist and a past professor of psychiatry and family medicine. She specializes in methods to access relational resilience for prevention, treatment, and long-term healing. She has devoted 50+ years to exploring the origins of addiction, mental health issues, and compulsions, and to facilitating long-term healing for individuals, families, and communities dealing with major challenges. She developed Transitional Family Therapy, the first integrative family therapy model, and its evidence-based protocols, including LIFE (Link Individual Family Empowerment), LINC Community Resilience, and ARISE® Comprehensive Care with Invitational Intervention®, for engagement, treatment, and long-term healing of individuals and their families struggling with chronic and life-threatening illnesses. She has authored several books, including *AIDS* and *Health and Mental Health*, winner of the international Choice Library award, and has written over 200 papers. She has taught in 90+ countries and trained several thousand people in TFT and protocols. She served as a consultant to CDC&P, NIDA, NIAAA, WHO, and several international governments. A senior Fulbright consultant, Dr. Landau is recipient of numerous awards, including the 2026 Mae Abraham Legacy award for a woman who has advanced the field of addiction and alcohol treatment; the American Association of Marriage and Family Therapy's 2025 Founding Award: Visionary Impact Award for shaping the field of systemic family therapy, and the 2005 Outstanding Contribution to the Field award; the American Family Therapy Academy's Innovative Contribution to Family Therapy; the Winter Leadership Symposium's Lifetime Achievement award; the Association of Intervention Specialists' Interventionist of the Year 2023; and the Harmony Foundation's Trailblazer award. She is a traditional African healer (Sangoma), committed to bridging the gap between modern medical science and traditional healing.

Charlene Connie Sparcino is a mental health counselor, hypnotherapist, and spiritual practitioner whose work integrates past life regression, clinical insight, and shamanic wisdom. After a long career in banking and administration, she recognized a deeper calling – to bring clarity to emotional and spiritual disorder and guide others toward healing. Her meticulous administrative background became the foundation for a new path rooted in interpersonal, transpersonal, and spiritual transformation. Her search for past life understanding led her to Dr. Judith Landau, a respected author and early pioneer of spiritually integrated therapeutic practice. Their collaboration illuminated the direction that ultimately shaped this book. Charlene later earned her clinical master's degree and became certified by the Accredited American Institute of Hypnotherapy in 1998, expanding her ability to support clients through both psychological and spiritual awakening. Guided by shamanic teachings and a lifelong commitment to spiritual awareness, Charlene helps clients access insight, healing, and renewed purpose. Her work and this book reflect her dedication to bridging the seen and unseen, the clinical and the mystical, and the past and the present.

Foreword by Steve Burgess

What an amazing difference I have seen over the last thirty-something years in my career as a Regression Therapist in the growth and credibility of Past Life Therapy (PLT)! After the ground-breaking and eye-opening work of Brian Weiss in his book "Many Lives, Many Masters," and through the extensive writings of Dolores Cannon, the subject of PLT has exploded in recent years as the growth of interest in reincarnation has blossomed. Few books, however, have been written from a clinical perspective, looking at how PLT can heal emotional and physical issues, so this book is all the more welcome as it is written by two of the most experienced regression therapists in the world.

Dr. Landau and Charlene Sparcino's brilliantly written and intelligently articulated book will cause anyone skeptical of the healing powers of PLT to reconsider their skepticism as they read of the transformations experienced by their clients.

As someone who has been a passionate advocate of regression therapy for all of my career, I am particularly pleased to see such an eminent and widely respected psychiatrist (Dr. Landau) and an experienced hypnotherapist (Charlene Sparcino) being prepared to promote PLT to a wider audience. I completely agree with the authors that Past Life Regression is an extremely effective therapeutic tool that needs to be considered with more respect by the psychotherapeutic community.

Not only is the book beautifully written but there is also a depth and profundity to some of the prose that highlights the often spiritual nature of regression into previous lifetimes. For example, the sentence from Chapter 3:

> Charlotte's plea for hypnotherapy brought her face to face with a reality that science could not measure, yet her soul could recognize

Those words stopped me in my tracks when I read them (I wish I had written them!) as they beautifully summarize the experience that so many of our clients have during their journeys into previous lives.

The wide-ranging nature of the cases which the authors share with us gives a good example of the breadth of issues that PLT can help with, and how refreshing it is to read the clients' own words of their experiences in trance, and the incredible ways in which their issues are healed, either through releasing the traumas in their past lives or through gaining deep understandings of how their experiences and relationships in former lifetimes have impacted them in their present life. As the authors write:

> (the clients)... 'experience provides an example of how identifying past traumas and behavior patterns can directly impact their lives in the present time. Becoming aware of this knowledge can disrupt these patterns and invoke resolution and change in behavior and circumstance in the present'.

Whether the issue being worked on is emotional, physical, or spiritual, PLT offers a way of healing at deeper levels than most other traditional therapy processes. Many negative behavior patterns or thought patterns stem from past life traumas, and the authors show that such patterns (which have been played out from life to life) usually dissolve away or, at the very least, become more flexible once they are regressed into and opened up in the therapy sessions. This means that the client regains some control over the old behaviors or thought processes, often for the first time in their lives, so they can remove the blocks that have been stopping them from living their lives freely and effectively.

However, the most unusual aspect presented in the book is the way in which Dr. Landau and Charlene Sparcino work with relationship issues within families, and this is something that I think is unique in the hypnotherapy world, that of guiding whole families or couples into past lives at the same time. Of course, Family Constellation Therapy will spring to mind, but the way in which the authors use regression within this dynamic is much deeper, as it is the family connections within their previous lives that help to create deep and effective healings for all concerned. I think you'll find this fascinating as you read the past life experiences and the understandings that come from the process.

Another unusual element is the stories of clients experiencing past lives as animals, and I applaud Dr. Landau and Charlene Sparcino's courage in sharing these stories, as this phenomenon is something which is easy to deride or belittle as simply being the imagination of the clients. In my work, I have also found occasionally that a client will relive a past life as an animal. It may be that they are simply imagining these experiences, but the most important thing is that the experience helps them to get better and to heal their issues, which it invariably does.

Commendably, the authors' care and compassion for their clients and their families shine through in the way that they keep them safe throughout the regression process, and the spiritual growth that the clients and their families experience is highlighted in each chapter. The authors make a compelling and intelligent case for PLT to be accepted more widely in the psychotherapeutic community.

Whether you're new to the concept of Past Life Regression, a therapist looking to expand your portfolio into the world of regression, or someone fascinated by the subject, prepare to be entertained, enthralled, and informed by a book which deservedly sits alongside "Many Lives, Many Masters" on any bookshelf.

Steve Burgess
Hypnotherapist and Regression Specialist
www.steveburgesshypnosis.com

Acknowledgments

Thank you to Pamela Ruth Landau Lessing and Allison Rebecca Naudé for their tireless editorial help on earlier versions of this book. Thank you also to Megen Musegades and Anne and Raoul Naudé for their significant comments. Our furry families have attempted to help with indelible editing, and we thank them for their intention and relentless support. Finally, our deep gratitude to our Editor, Hannah Rich, and Editorial Assistant, Pragati Sharma. Without all of them, this book might never have made it to press.

Introduction

Invitation to the Other Side of Time

Have you ever stepped beyond the seam of this world?
I think I drifted there once,
or perhaps I dreamt it.
The air was thin with remembering,
and everything shimmered as if it had just been born.

Author

This book does not ask the reader to adopt a particular belief about past lives, reincarnation, or spiritual ontology. It asks something both simpler and more demanding: to consider how meaning, memory, relationship, and unacknowledged history shape lives, and how healing becomes possible when those forces are witnessed.

Throughout these chapters, Past Life Regression Hypnotherapy is used as a clinical and experiential framework for accessing meaning. Whether the material that emerges is understood as literal memory, symbolic narrative, metaphor, imagination, or embodied experience is ultimately less important than its effect. What heals is not proof of the past, but coherence in the present and hope for the future. Symptoms soften when their story is heard. Fear loosens when experience is shared. Choice emerges where compulsion once ruled.

The work presented here is grounded in ethical, collaborative care. Several of the individuals whose stories you will encounter live with serious medical and psychiatric conditions and continue to require ongoing treatment. Past Life Regression Hypnotherapy is not offered as a replacement for science-based care, but as a companion to it, one that can deepen understanding, restore agency, and support resilience when used with humility and clinical responsibility.

What follows is both a personal and professional journey. It is not intended as a declaration of belief, but as context for why this work emerged, how it has been practiced, and what it has made possible for patients, families, and clinicians.

DOI: 10.4324/9781003636182-1

Judith's Story

My awareness of a spiritual bond with my father began with my very first memory when I was about nine months old. He carried me outside in his arms to see a brilliant sunrise. In that moment, vague flashes of memory and past lives were illuminated. I knew that our connection transcended time. Throughout my life, including during several near-death experiences, the bond with my father gave me a sense of safety and continuity.

Every so often, I have other amazing experiences of recognition when seeing or sensing someone from my distant past. It might take me days, weeks, months, or even years for the memory to resurface, and then I have the realization: We have been together before. What follows are some of these experiences that I hope will provide you with an understanding of why I decided to write this book.

When I was three years old, I remember hearing my mother tell a close friend, "We've lost Eve!" Her friend burst into tears, and they held each other for a very long time. Eve, the baby sister of one of my good friends, had become seriously ill with diphtheria.[1] The epidemic affected many of the children in our area, most of whom had not been immunized. Almost all these children died, and Eve was one of the first that I knew to succumb. My parents tried to hide this from me, but I was aware from all the whispers and secrecy that something dreadful was happening. They felt helpless, and I knew that somehow, I was involved. Was there something I should or could have done? The question haunted me for many years.

One morning, a little while after Eve's death, I woke with a very sore throat. My throat was closing. I was gasping for breath. I was suffocating and very frightened. I did not understand what was happening to me, nor why I remembered the pediatrician arriving and saying, "Don't be frightened, I am just going to clear your throat with this swab so you can breathe." The swab stick looked very long and threatening. Much later, I discovered the full story of that night. The tip of the swab had come off, dropped down my throat, and entered my lung, making it impossible for me to breathe. What I personally remembered was riding in an ambulance with the doctor, but I had no idea where my parents were. I felt small and helpless.

In that same memory, the next thing I saw was me floating above myself. I was in an operating room, watching as doctors using large instruments worked on my immobile body. Rather than being scared, I felt an all-encompassing feeling of peace and warmth as I left this life and crossed over to the other side. I was met by three female figures in diaphanous, long, white robes. They seemed thrilled to see me, and I sensed a joy because I felt I was coming 'Home.' Somehow, I knew them. I was back with people who loved me, and whom I loved. There was nothing but light and joy. These figures enveloped me. I felt a sense of utter peace. I never wanted to leave. I was with my 'Guides' and for a short while one of them held me, filling me with an incredible sense of belonging and connection. She then said very firmly, "Before you come home, turn around and look at your parents." Then I saw them. They were standing in the back of the operating room, devastated, and weeping as they watched the limp body of their tiny daughter dying on the operating table.

While I looked at them, one of my other 'Guides' asked, "Do you remember why you chose this life? You haven't even started your work yet." I knew I had contributions to make in this lifetime. I was also flooded with an awareness and love of my parents, and I felt their overwhelming pain. Without another moment's thought, I rushed back into my body.

At that moment, I remembered why I had chosen them as my parents. It was because they were making a huge difference in the world. My father was a light-bearer. He was ready to sacrifice himself completely for the good of humanity: for health, justice, and equality. My mother was strong, intelligent, generous, loving, and determined. These people, my parents, would help me frame a lifetime of work that was ahead of me.

Back in my body, I felt an incredible sense of relief as I took my first unlabored breath since getting diphtheria. My parents were next to me, and I watched them collapse into each other's arms when they saw me breathing on my own. This was my first conscious near-death experience. Because I had been immunized, I was one of the lucky few who survived.

My next significant, lifetime challenge was being in a glass isolation booth to avoid contaminating others with the radiation I was receiving as treatment for the diphtheria.[2] I was entirely alone, unable to talk to anyone or have visitors. My time in the booth felt interminable! I missed my parents and didn't understand why they weren't allowed to be with me. Was I a danger to them? Would they catch my infection and die? I remember being there, wishing that I could go back to the warmth and safety of the other side that I had so recently chosen to leave.

The 'Guide' who had held me earlier, Akwane, suddenly reappeared and said, "My child, we have always been here and will always be here when you need us. You can come and visit us whenever you choose." It was that significant moment and those special words that changed my life because I have never again felt entirely alone. It was a reminder of the many times that she and I had been together through both good and bad past life experiences.

The morning after returning home from the irradiation, I was unable to move my legs, a paralysis[3] caused by the diphtheria. I have vivid memories of lying on the raised porch watching my friends play below. I remember the sensation of watching them play and seeing myself involved in the game. It was the first time that I realized that I could detach from my body and watch a scene without being emotionally involved. This is a skill that I have used many times since then, and one that is extremely useful to my patients during their hypnotherapy.

When I was five, I was playing on the beach when a freak wave pulled me under the water. I was not frightened but rather felt a strange sense of peace in the darkness. Later, I learned that I had had another "near death experience." My father dove into the water to rescue me, and I watched from above as he worked frantically to resuscitate my lifeless body.

While young, I had vague memories and saw flashbacks of other places, times, and people from the past, long ago. However, I did not feel connected to any of these experiences. When I was anxious or fearful, I knew I could leave a situation at will, go to a safe place, and find my Guides. This meant that I always had a sense of relief because I knew I was safe.

I had never kept secrets from my parents, but from my visits to the 'Other Side,' I knew that I needed to keep some things private. My new sense of purpose might not be acceptable to most of the people around me, even my parents. I found it a struggle to be true to myself, and I also understood the importance of keeping other people comfortable.

Another important experience led me to recognizing some of my spiritual gifts. As a five-year-old, I was visiting one of my father's health and community centers when the other children (all Zulu) asked me to go with them to a ceremony with the Isangoma, their spiritual healer. (The Isangoma is the spiritual healer of the tribe and is the preliminary judge of wrongdoing. Only if she cannot resolve the problem does it escalate to the Chief and his Council.) I wanted to go because I was fascinated, but I was also a little afraid because I knew that she was all-powerful and could see into the past and the future.

We sat behind the Isangoma, who was in a circle of women. She withdrew bones and herbs from the pouches hanging among her garments, hides, and beads. As she listened to the accusations, she threw the bones on the ground, observing the pattern they made. She then threw herbs into the fire, and shapes emerged. Without understanding why, I recognized the innocence of the accused. Bursting with excitement, I blurted out, "she didn't kill him, she wasn't even there!" The Isangoma gently silenced me and asked me to stay after the ceremony. When we were alone, she told me, very seriously, that I had inherited .... and with it, a huge responsibility. I was an Isangoma. It was this knowledge, its privilege and its burden, that formed my commitment to bridge traditional healing and modern science.

My father died of a massive heart attack when I was six years old. This left my mother with a one-month-old baby boy and me, as her sole emotional support. She had a full-time job and could only afford a nanny in the mornings. I needed to race home from school to take care of an infant, and I was only six! The responsibility was overwhelming. I remember wishing that there were divine beings who could be there to help me manage my life.

It was during one of those desperate prayers for help that Akwane – tall, slender, and dressed in her diaphanous robe – suddenly appeared beside my bed. I remembered that she had greeted me when I 'crossed over' during my battle with diphtheria, and during the loneliness of my subsequent radiation. Among my Guides her presence was unmistakable. Twice before, it was she who had asked me whether I was truly ready to return 'Home.' This was the third of many visits. Her presence helped me harness my connection to the 'Other Side' and reinforced my knowledge that I was not alone. To this day, she has remained a constant source of inspiration, accountability, and humility. These and other experiences solidified my belief in the connection between this world and other(s), and the continuity of souls. This was the beginning of a series of extraordinary experiences.

Many years later, already a physician, I was flooded with memories of another encounter with Akwane. In that lifetime, I was the primary healer for one of the Ethiopian Nilotic peoples who preceded the Maasai.[4] Akwane had been my closest friend and helper. When a devastating disease (possibly rinderpest[5]) decimated the cattle herds, it left our people starving. None of my efforts could save us.

Akwane came to me as I wept, attempting to reassure me that I had done my best. She reminded me about my previous medical issues and how my doctors, using the medical knowledge of the time, had saved me but left me with the many consequences of their failures. I knew that my treatments for diphtheria, at the age of three, left me with a weakened immune system, which resulted in multiple cancers and other illnesses. With her guidance, I understood that these experiences were all very similar. In this lifetime, I had lived through multiple iatrogenic diseases that were not caused by the failure of the doctors who treated me, but the lack of knowledge at that time (Weigensberg, et al., 1984). For the first time, I was able to see that I too had done my best for my people, and so I could begin the process of self-forgiveness.

The Hippocratic oath and the commitment to first "do no harm" have been my guiding principles throughout my career. This realization that I did not intentionally cause harm has helped me forgive myself for my failures as a healer (iatros) in my past lives.[6]

As a second-year medical student, aged 17, I was trained to do hypnosis. This was another pivotal experience in my life. Under stress, many people are unable to share their feelings with family members, whether because of cultural, family, or personal pressures. These people, typically young and female, would present in the Emergency Room with extreme somatic expressions of such distress. This included dissociative paralysis, deafness, or blindness. Previously, this was called "hysteria" and was seen as an expression of extreme emotional distress accompanied by a feeling of helplessness. Hypnosis was an effective method for bringing such patients out of their dissociative state.

Each time I hypnotized a young woman and watched her regain her capacity to move, to see, or to hear, I was awed by the experience. I began to ask the person, "What did you feel, see, or hear while I was treating you?" One woman reported, "I was back in my bedroom dreading the appearance of my husband and his demands for intimacy. He hurts me without any awareness of what he's doing. He never asks how I feel. I am too ashamed of not enjoying the experience to tell him the truth. He would send me back to my parents for not being a good enough bride. The shame would be the end of my life."

Another patient, an older woman, revealed that she was being severely beaten by her mother-in-law, who ran the household. She tried to tell her husband, but he was dubious about her stories and powerless to help her. I treated many others who were also being abused by their husbands. These women shared the sense that they had no recourse, but that they were trapped in their current situations forever. I started searching for a common thread, something that would provide an answer to an apparent situation. It was only years later that I realized that I was being led, in very small steps, toward a pathway I could never have imagined.

One of the young women, Parveena, whose family had recently immigrated from New Delhi, India, to Durban, South Africa, came to the appointment with four of her family members. Parveena was a 15-year-old patient who had been unable to walk for several weeks. I had noticed that many of the patients came to the hospital with several family members, so this did not surprise me. They were typically asked to sit in the waiting room while the patients were examined. Knowing this, I asked my new patient, Parveena, whether any of her family was with her. She said her mother, grandmother, maternal aunt, and older brother had brought her to the hospital. With her permission, I invited them to join us in the examination room.

As soon as the hypnosis started, Parveena began to describe herself in the third person, "She is walking down a narrow mountain path. It is dangerous. I'm worried for her. She is weeping about having to leave home to marry a stranger." I asked who she was. She answered, "I think women were talking about another past life experience as though they were all in it together. They had all been sisters and had been seriously beaten, raped, and ultimately murdered by their father. They were all sobbing and comforting one another.

I asked them, "*On a count of 5, please go back in time to when you were all living together in the mountains and walking along the mountain path to the wedding.*" With that, they were all back together with the 12-year-old bride as she started her wedding journey. And her current family could see themselves as her mother, oldest brother, and uncle. Mother burst into tears, saying, "I can't do this to my child! I don't want her beaten like me. I don't know what to do."

When I brought them out of their hypnotic state, we were able to process the experience and talk openly about how trapped her mother had been as a young girl when she herself had been forced to marry. She wept about how helpless she felt about protecting her daughter, both then and now. Parveena's grandmother said stoically, "We had no voice."

Clearly, this was a repetition of a previous time in their lives. The Past Life Regression Hypnotherapy experience provided them with an opportunity to recognize their roles as women in this lifetime. Parveena started to talk openly with her mother and her older brother about her fear that she would be forced into an arranged marriage. Her family acknowledged the cultural shift that was happening across generations and reassured her that she would be involved in the decision. Unintentionally, this was the beginning of my first Past Life Regression Hypnotherapy with a patient and her family, rather than the patient alone.

My experience with hypnotherapy as a medical student, combined with my personal past life experiences and my identity as a healer, led me to the exciting mission of bridging the two worlds of modern medicine and traditional healing.

Years later, as a neuropsychiatrist, family therapist, and Jungian analyst, I discovered I was not alone in this calling to support individuals and families through past life regression. With my training in Jungian analysis and my experience with dissociative symptoms, I had read one of the earliest and most powerful books, "*Other Lives, Other Selves*" by a Jungian analyst, Woolger (1988). He drew attention to the psychology of reincarnation and the dramatic power of past life regression to radically transform and heal our lives. I was drawn to explore the concept further.

Another key event was discovering an upcoming conference on Past Life Regression Hypnotherapy, where the renowned Dr. Brian Weiss would be speaking. Others were clearly providing a similar service, and I couldn't wait to meet them.

The night before the conference, I woke up and found myself in someone else's dream. I was rescuing him from marauding animals. I completed the rescue and went back to sleep, thinking no more about it. The next morning, in the breakfast buffet line, I was tapped on the shoulder, and there was my nighttime visitor, Brian Weiss, thanking me for the rescue![7]

During the conference, we were able to spend quite a bit of time together and subsequently became good friends and colleagues.

Dr. Weiss and I worked very differently but had a great deal in common. I particularly loved his first book, *Many Lives, Many Masters*, and have thoroughly enjoyed his others (Weiss, 1988). The fact that we were both neuropsychiatrists, and his openness to learning from the "Other Side," was very important to me.

During my exploration of others involved in the same search, a colleague introduced me to the writings of Jane Roberts (1972), an upstate New York neighbor. Her stories inspired me further. The special gift from my wife of a first edition of A.R. Martin's (1942) groundbreaking book, "Researches in Reincarnation and Beyond," was another inspiration. These readings had a profound influence on my approach to medicine and spirituality.

Throughout my career as a physician, teacher, researcher, and healer, I have focused my work on resilience. I carry with me an innate sense of *Ubuntu. Ubuntu* means that we are ourselves because we are part of a community. We can only be whole when we consider not only ourselves and our families but all the people in our context.[8] This is a prevalent African philosophy that guides behavior at a profound level and forms the foundation of our work. A key tenet arising from this is the belief that all individuals, families, and communities are inherently resilient and competent (Landau, 2018).

Exploring experiences that arise in regression, whether understood as past lives, symbolic narratives, embodied memory, or expressions of the collective unconscious, can help individuals understand who they have been and who they are becoming (Jung, 1991). It can also help us understand why we are here now and what we need to achieve during this lifetime. We hope that this chapter excites you and has you yearning to know who you were, who you are, and why you are here.

Not all readers will believe that these experiences represent literal past lives. That belief is not required. Perhaps these chapters are just interesting stories, and you can enjoy them as such. For many years, I thought that my experiences were just a metaphor, perhaps inspired by Carl Jung's (1991) concept of the Collective Unconscious. What matters is that this approach offers another way of listening to the body, to memory, to relationships, and another tool for supporting troubled individuals and their families.

The names, places, and all identifying information of the individuals and families who have shared their stories with us have been changed to prevent them from being identified and to protect their anonymity. I trust that they will be comfortable with their "modified" stories as we have shared them.

For those of you who are interested in learning more about our method, the details may be found in the Appendix: Past Life Regression Hypnotherapy: 'Place of Joy.'

Notes

1 Diphtheria kills people because a white membrane grows across the throat from the infection and strangles people to death. In Afrikaans, it is called "wit seer keel," or "white sore throat."
2 The prevailing medical belief was that the thymus was the seat of infection, and with serious infectious disease, it needed to be eradicated by radiation. The patient was completely isolated until the radiation dissipated to avoid exposing visitors to irradiation.
3 Peripheral neuropathy, a rare complication of diphtheria.
4 Nilotic Tribes (Ehret, 2001; Bender, 1997). Long before there were written records, Nilotic peoples apparently migrated from the Nile River area as far south as the region of modern Tanzania. Some Nilotic groups had intensive contact with Cushitic (Afro-Asiatic) peoples, and with Niger-Congo peoples. This has resulted in mutual cultural and linguistic impact across Nilotic, Cushitic, and Niger-Congo language families.
5 Rinderpest (cattle plague) was a devastating, highly contagious viral disease of cloven-hoofed animals. Through a massive vaccination campaign, it was eradicated in 2011 (Donald, 2011).
6 At that time, the prevailing belief was that the thymus gland was responsible for infection, so eradicating it with radiation was believed to be the appropriate cure for life-threatening infections such as diphtheria. We now know that the thymus is responsible for immunity, and a very high percentage of those children around the world who had their thymus irradiated have developed multiple cancers of the head, neck, and skin as a result.
7 Brian Weiss, personal communication.
8 Ubuntu (Nguni language) is defined by a person's relations with other people. "I am because you are: Without you I am not a person." Ubuntu refers to behaving well toward others or acting in ways that benefit the community. A person who behaves in these ways has Ubuntu. He or she is a full person.

Chapter 1

Living With Shadows

What we bury does not sleep; it hums beneath our waking.
To walk in light is to carry our shadows wisely,
not banished but understood.

Author

Charlotte, a 37-year-old professional, sought help after months of torment. Her long-term domestic partner, Jill, and her other family members were unable to hear the noises she described, and she began to fear for her sanity. Medical doctors labeled her condition 'psychotic auditory hallucinations and delusions,' and prescribed multiple medications, none of which eased her distress.[1]

When Charlotte came to see us, she was exhausted both emotionally and spiritually. She told us how, throughout the night, she heard the scraping sound of metal on stone, machines turning on and off, and the crackling sound of fire. She got no sleep and woke exhausted each morning. She was extremely anxious and had almost given up any hope of health and healing. Her first comment was, "If this doesn't work, I don't know what will." As we embarked on the Past Life Regression Hypnotherapy journey, it became clear to all of us that this was the approach she needed.

In this chapter, we explore Charlotte's journey, a woman tormented by sounds that no one else could hear. Diagnosed as psychotic and treated unsuccessfully with medication, Charlotte's plea for Past Life Regression Hypnotherapy brought her face-to-face with a reality that science could not measure, yet her soul could recognize. What unfolded next would forever shift her treatment team's understanding of healing and the unseen layers of consciousness. There are moments when the boundaries between mind and spirit blur; when what appears as madness may, in truth, be memories.[2]

DOI: 10.4324/9781003636182-2

Charlotte's Story

For years, I lived with sounds no one else could hear. Footsteps pacing my hallway at night. A low whisper behind the bedroom wall. Sudden thuds that made my entire body jump. And then there was the one that broke me – a persistent, steady hum that I felt inside my soul. No one else heard it. My family thought I was imagining things. My doctor said it was psychosis and prescribed pills that dulled everything, my feelings, my mind, my thoughts, but never the sounds.

The medications wove themselves into every hour of my day and every corner of my night. Sleep became something I remembered, not something I experienced. By the time I met Judith, I was ready to give up. I didn't want to die. I just wanted it to stop. I wanted silence.

My life partner, Jill, came with me to that first session. She sat beside me, her hand wrapped around mine, eyes filled with worry and love.

She said to Judith, "I just want her to feel safe again." I remember thinking how far away "safe" felt to me.

I told them, "Normal feels like a foreign word. All I know is the exhaustion of fear, the longing for silence, and the ache for my home to feel like mine again. I want to feel like a human being with a future."

To reassure me and help me feel safe in her space, Judith began by working on progressive relaxation exercises. It took me two sessions and homework each night before I was able to reach a state of relaxation. She also asked Jill to work on these exercises so that when we were ready to be hypnotized, she could be right there with me. I was excited and ready to start this journey into my past.

As our next session began, Judith asked me to imagine a safe place that would become my 'Place of Joy.' I closed my eyes and saw my childhood bedroom; lace curtains glowing with morning sun, my cat curled on the windowsill, the faint smell of pancakes drifting up from the kitchen. That memory became my anchor. I chanted it to myself like a prayer: *You are safe. You are safe. You are safe.* Every time the terror crept back in, I held onto it like a rope that could lead me home.

Once Jill and I were both relaxed, Judith felt we were ready to embark on hypnotherapy. She asked us the way in which we would like to move into the past. She suggested that we might choose to walk down a pathway to a gate, or float into the clouds, or climb toward the top of a mountain. She assured us that the pathway we chose would be the right one for us and that there were no mistakes that we could make during this process. She told Jill that she was welcome to find her own 'Place of Joy' or just share in Charlotte's experience. Jill said that, at this stage, she preferred to be an observer but agreed to let us both know if she changed her mind.

When we began the hypnotherapy, Judith's voice was calm and steady. "*Close your eyes,*" she said. "*Take a deep breath. You are safe. You may see something long forgotten, and that is okay. If at any point this is too much, I will help you float up and out of your body so you can watch from a safe place and not feel the fear.*"

She then said, "*I'd like you to let your body rest as your mind begins to wander back to the very first moment these sounds began. What do you notice? What do you see, sense, smell or hear?*"

"It's dark... I can hear something scraping, metal on stone. It's the same sound that's been following me. Only now I can *see* it."

Judith continued to reassure me, "*You're doing beautifully, Charlotte. Stay with what's unfolding. What's happening around you?*"

"I'm... not me. I'm someone else. I'm in a small room with stone walls. It's cold. I think I'm in a prison cell. There's a chain dragging on the floor... that's the noise! That's it!"

Judith's voice was reassuring, "*Very good. Look down at your feet. What do you see?*"

"Bare feet. Dirt. My clothes are rough, torn. I was accused of something. I didn't do it. They're coming for me again... I can hear the guard!"

I heard Judith say, "*You're safe here. Float up to the ceiling and watch the scene from above where you can see, hear, and observe everything without feeling the pain. That was then, and this is now. Allow yourself to observe, not relive the experience. What happens next?*"

"He's coming in. He's angry. He thinks I'm hiding something. He hits me. I fall... my head hurts... everything is silent. I must have died. And now it's peaceful. I'm floating above. But I still hear the chains. I thought I'd never be free."

Judith's interjected, "*Now, from this place of awareness, let's bring light to that memory. Tell the part of you that's still there that you can release the noise. You're free now.*"

At that moment, I knew, "I forgive him. I forgive myself for holding on. The scraping sound is fading... it's gone."

During our second hypnotherapy session, I reported that I no longer heard the scraping sound but was still being woken throughout the night by the constant sound of a machine and the crackle of fire. I reported that I was feeling better, but still not getting the sleep I needed.

My second hypnotherapy induction began with Judith counting... The room around me faded, and suddenly, I am three years old.

"I am crouched behind a heavy refrigerator on a wooden porch. I recognize the sound of many of my troubled nights. My hands are pressed against the cold metal. The air smells like damp wood and smoke. I hear scraping, screams, loud voices, and terrible dull thuds. My little body freezes. I peek out and see shadows moving, and then I see my beloved father lying absolutely still on the floor. He is in a pool of blood. My heart is pounding so fast I think it will burst. I want to run, but I can't."

Judith's voice reached me again, telling me to float upward. I lifted out of my small body, up toward the ceiling. From above, I saw everything: the chaos, my beloved father lying bleeding on the floor, and my mother gone. I had no idea when she left, where she went, or when if ever she would return. I was completely alone. I watched the little girl looking bereft and I tried to find words of comfort, but none came to me.

As Judith counted slowly backward from ten to one, the scene disappeared. I felt the chair under me again. I opened my eyes, shaking, and saw Jill holding my hand. I was here. I was safe. I could almost see the scene that I had just experienced, but it was fading fast and losing its intensity.

Judith asked both of us to write down what we remembered from this session. For days, images and feelings came and went. Some were mine; others felt older, heavier, like memories passed down through blood.

Our next session focused on debriefing. Jill and I had been instructed not to talk about our memories of the session, but to share them in our journals in preparation for the next session that would focus on debriefing. We were also asked to write about all that we could remember about our dreams, thoughts, and memories that came up after the session. Even though Jill had not participated in the hypnosis, we had been told that she might have relevant thoughts and dreams arising from the process, and this proved to be the case. She had been having vivid, repeating dreams in which she rescued me from a group of gangsters. She felt that these might have been dreams about a past life with me. We agreed to explore that once I was doing better.

Our next hypnotherapy session was different. I was older and the scene was different: A city was burning, people were screaming, and buildings were collapsing. I saw myself holding a small child and shielding him in my arms. My whole body was shaking, but I couldn't run.

I said, "I am trying to remind myself; *I can choose where to put my attention.*" Even in the chaos, I realized I was not powerless. I had a responsibility to this small soul, and I was determined to find the strength to survive for both our sakes.

After the session, Jill told me that she had squeezed my hand while I was in the hypnotic state. She said, "I wanted you to feel that you weren't alone." I believe I did feel her presence strongly.

In another regression session, I saw myself as a young teenage boy, hiding in a dim room from people in authority who were threatening me with punishment. My closest friend, James, was right there with me, a lone support in a terrifying situation. Together we stood firm as the threats increased. I was terrified. All that stood between me and those threatening us was James' firm hand that I clutched.

As I tried to work out how to escape, Judith's reassuring voice said, *"Float out of your body and go to a place where you are safe and happy, your 'Place of Joy.'"*

I was able to float away and reach my 'Place of Joy.' This nightmare was over. More importantly, I realized that James in that lifetime was my dear Jill in this one.

It was after that session, and during the nightmares that followed for many nights, that I finally understood the sounds that had haunted me all my life. They weren't madness; they were memories. They were echoes of fear trapped in time. I realized that I had a choice. I could continue to live with the fear or let it go!

I spoke softly to that teenage boy I once had been, "You did the best you could. You survived. You are safe now."

I repeated the message to all the souls I had also been. Something inside me seemed to soften. I started to feel a level of compassion and understanding of their situation, and therefore an understanding of myself. None of this was my fault. I wasn't crazy, I had just lived through terrifying times and been threatened by dangerous people and situations.

Over the next few sessions, I began to feel differently about the sounds. They weren't delusions. They were pieces of my story, fragments of trauma trying to find their way home. I started to hold them in my mind and heart with compassion instead of fear. For the first time in months, I could breathe deeply without bracing for the next noise. The shadows didn't vanish, but they stopped ruling me. They were no longer in charge; I was.

Jill said something to me one night that I'll never forget. After one of the old terrifying nightmares, as she held me tightly and soothed me, she looked at me and said, "When I whisper to you in the night, 'I see you now,' it is more than comfort. It is truth. I finally understand that what you carry is real."

That was when I knew we were healing, not by erasing the past, but by standing inside it together, strong enough to withstand any threat, provided we faced it together.

Now, my house was quiet in the way it was supposed to be. I slept through the night. The air felt soft again. I still remembered the sounds, but they didn't own me anymore. I carried the memory, but it didn't carry me.

Every morning, I told the little girl inside me, "You are safe. You are loved. You belong."

Jill said our home felt warmer now. Maybe it did. Maybe healing was less about silence and more about listening, really listening, to what was once too painful to hear. I used to think I was losing my mind. Now I understood I was remembering it. The whispers, the hum, the crackle of fire, the footsteps, they weren't signs of madness. They were pieces of truth waiting to be heard. Healing, I've learned, isn't the absence of fear. It's the courage to face it with compassion, with patience, with love. It's the moment you turn toward the darkness and tell yourself, "I see you," and the shadows finally begin to fade.

Over the following weeks, the noises did not return. My family, once fearful and confused, found themselves drawn into my healing process with awe and renewed faith in the mysteries of the human spirit.

Even my psychiatrist, though skeptical, admitted, "Whatever you did, it worked." It took several months before I felt safe enough to reduce my antipsychotic medication, and my psychiatrist worked with me on a gradual reduction plan until I was completely off all medication.

Reader Takeaway

This story shows us that not every hallucination is necessarily psychosis. Charlotte's story invites us to question how we define "reality." Not every unexplained experience is psychosis, nor is every noise a haunting. Was this psychosis that healed gradually as Charlotte gained faith and understanding in herself? Sometimes, what haunts us is the unhealed fragment of our own soul echoing across time until it is finally acknowledged and released. What emerges as fear, threats, or shadows may be the echo of trauma across lifetimes, seeking to be witnessed, integrated, and held.

Healing isn't always linear or limited to the current lifetime. The body remembers, even when the conscious mind cannot. By honoring the story beneath the symptom, we gave Charlotte's soul a voice. Healing becomes possible when patients and families meet these echoes with openness rather than dismissal.

Charlotte's journey reminds us that symptoms do not always equal illness. What looks like madness may be memory; what feels like haunting may be unspoken history surfacing. When modern medicine reaches its limits, it's often a signal that the spirit is asking to be heard, a voice that traditional healers always listen for. We must remember that healing is not confined to the mind. It expands through the body, the spirit, and even the lifetimes that shape us. Past life regression offers us a bridge between science and spirit, a way to listen deeply, not only to what our clients say, but to what their souls are trying to remember.

This chapter shows us that resilience is not the absence of fear, but the ability to face it with compassion, integration, and trust. Healing lies in the courage to witness pain, the patience to hold space for what arises, and the love that transforms shadows into connection and leads to freedom from pain and fear.

Would Charlotte's psychotic symptoms have been reduced over time and with regular appointments with her psychiatrist? We may never know the answer, but we do know that the collaborative work resolved her symptoms and allowed her to stop taking medication. A strong collaborative team can help treat illness efficiently and quickly. In this instance, Charlotte's return to a productive life was accelerated by the addition of Past Life Regression Hypnotherapy.

Notes

1 Psychosis: In clinical psychiatry, psychosis is a broad term describing experiences such as hallucinations, delusions, and altered perceptions of reality. Contemporary trauma research increasingly recognizes that not all psychosis-like experiences arise from primary psychotic disorders, and that trauma, dissociation, and meaning-making processes can significantly influence symptom presentation.

2 Trauma-Encoded Imagery: Trauma-encoded imagery refers to sensory, emotional, or symbolic material that emerges from unprocessed traumatic experiences. Such imagery may appear intrusive, vivid, or externalized and can resemble hallucinations, particularly when early-life or overwhelming trauma has not been consciously integrated.

Chapter 2

Will the Pain Ever Stop?

> Chronic pain often endures not because it cannot be healed, but because it has not yet been understood.
>
> Author

Natalie's story began not with the ache in her back, but with a silent suffering that had persisted over decades. Natalie, a 42-year-old woman, had, for as long as she could remember, been troubled by incessant chronic pain in her lower back. It interfered with her sleep, prevented her from being able to complete simple routine daily tasks, and resulted in her losing several jobs. She had given up attempting to obtain a diagnosis and was in despair. Her days were shadowed by a dull, relentless ache that refused to wane, no matter the treatment or her behavior.

Natalie's family was very close-knit and built around traditional values, where resilience was prized, and stoicism was often mistaken for strength. The cultural fabric of the family emphasized endurance, perseverance, and a sense of collective responsibility; traits that served her well in life but also created barriers for expressing vulnerability or seeking help for emotional distress. Her primary relationship was with her husband, James, who had become her confidante and partner in the hope of finding relief.

James had grown up in a family that was more open about their emotions than Natalie's, and she was comfortable sharing her despair with him. Over years of her suffering, they had navigated a maze of medical assessments, herbal remedies, and alternative healers, none yielding concrete answers. Her pain was so entrenched that she often wondered if she was cursed, or if perhaps her suffering was karmic. Could her chronic pain reflect some unseen debt from a previous life and a divine reckoning for these past deeds? Such questions haunted her and fueled feelings of helplessness and despair.

DOI: 10.4324/9781003636182-3

Natalie's Story

For as long as I could remember, I suffered from relentless pain in my lower back. It interfered with my sleep and prevented my doing simple routine daily tasks. I lost several jobs. No matter what treatment I tried, the dull, relentless ache refused to lessen. I had almost given up attempting to obtain a diagnosis and was in despair. Then I heard about Past Life Regression Hypnotherapy and wondered whether it might help.

At the beginning of my first session with Judith, I felt very tense and anxious despite my husband, James, tightly holding my hand. I was reluctant to share how bad the pain was and how hopeless I felt in case Judith confirmed my fear that this would be a permanent state.

She started by asking me, "*Tell me what brought you here today?*" I hesitated for a moment before replying. I feared that she would say that she couldn't help me, and my decision to consult her would reveal my secrets without providing hope of a solution.

I reluctantly shared, "I've had this pain in my lower back for as long as I can remember. Nothing seems to help, and I just want to understand why I'm like this. I want to find relief, not just for my body but for my mind, too."

James added, "We're both exhausted. We've tried so many things, doctors, herbalists, even alternative healers, but nothing sticks. Mostly, I just want her to be free from this pain, whatever it takes."

Judith responded, "*It's clear that your primary goal is to find relief from the physical pain, but I also sense there's a deeper longing for understanding. Perhaps you both have a need to grasp why this has happened and how it can be changed. Does that sound accurate?*"

I replied, "Yes, I just want peace. I want to wake up and feel like I can do everything again without this constant ache holding me back. Sometimes, I wonder if I'll have to live like this forever."

James reached over and took my hand gently and said, "We're both looking for a way forward. We need to find something physical, emotional, or spiritual, or maybe even just spiritual, that can help her heal from within. We're both willing to try anything. Our primary goal is to understand, to heal, and to discover if true relief is possible."

Our first session focused on Judith's teaching us the basics of progressive relaxation, which she encouraged us to practice daily in preparation for our hypnotherapy sessions. She also asked us to think about places where we had been happy either together or apart, a 'Place of Joy,' so that we could imagine them during our work with her. Judith explained that memories serve as vital anchors in therapy, especially in hypnosis. She said that it helps people achieve a sense of calm and inner strength amidst emotional turbulence and distress. She explained she would do a parallel session with James later, before working with us together in hypnotherapy. We both looked forward to our next meeting.

At our next session, my first hypnotherapy session, Judith asked me to close my eyes for a moment and to remember a moment, a time, or a place where I felt truly happy, safe, and most like me.

A scene immediately came to mind. I remembered being in my grandmother's garden. It was a sunny afternoon, and the air smelled like roses and fresh earth. There was a big old oak tree with moss hanging from its branches. My siblings and I were running around, laughing and picking flowers. My grandmother was there too, smiling and telling stories. I felt completely at peace, like everything was right in the world.

Judith asked me to hold onto that feeling and asked, "*Can you describe what you see, hear, feel, or even smell there?*"

I saw the bright blue sky, heard the birds singing, and felt the warmth of the sun on my skin. The scent of flowers made me feel carefree, and I remembered the sound of her voice, so gentle, telling us stories about our ancestors. Judith asked me to hold on to this memory as an anchor in order to counter potentially distressful memories and to access my inner resilience.

"*Whenever you feel overwhelmed*," she explained, "*you can return to this place in your mind, imagine yourself under that oak tree, feeling safe and loved. It's your sanctuary, your power spot where healing begins, your 'Place of Joy.'*"

In subsequent hypnotherapy sessions, when I revisited my grandmother's garden, I knew that I was in a place where I could breathe freely, where I was just me, not the woman with pain, but a girl who was happy and safe.

Then Judith guided me into a deeper, relaxed state of hypnosis. I was aware of my breath slowing, my muscles softening, and I felt myself drifting into a tranquil state. Judith prompted me to revisit my grandmother's garden, my 'Place of Joy.'

I was there almost instantly, and I could see and feel myself in the bright sunshine with the scent of flowers and my grandmother's soothing voice. Judith asked me to hold that wonderful feeling and move back in time to a place of significance related to my pain. She counted slowly, "*one... two... three... four...*" and clicked her fingers. Then, in a quiet, soft voice, she said, "*Feel the ground beneath your feet, the air on your body, and hear the sounds around you.*"

"I am in bright sunshine. I can hear leaves rustling and the sound of birds calling." I heard Judith say, "*Look at yourself. What do you see?*"

"I see a tall Zulu warrior, proud and strong. I'm young, confident, holding my spear. My wife Tembisa and my son Kagiso are nearby at our camp. I feel powerful and protective. They trust me. I can see the lion we just hunted on the ground nearby. There is still blood on my hands. I can feel the strength in my body. It is wonderful! My friends are here with me, and we are going to drink the lion's blood together to celebrate. I am very proud of myself and can't wait to tell Tembisa and Kagiso about the successful hunt."

"Suddenly, I see things changing. I hear young men from another tribe rushing towards us. I'm worried that we can't run fast enough to get away from them. I feel a sharp stab in my back and excruciating pain. It must be a spear. It feels as though it's still there. The pain is overwhelming and intense."

My vision of this life continued. "I feel my best friend holding my hand. He is shouting out for help. He says he'll run as fast as he can to bring help, but it is too late and I feel myself fading away. I ask him to run to Tembisa and Kagiso to tell them what is happening and I make him promise to take care of them if I don't make it back to camp. He races off and I know this is the end...I hear the warriors all around me, the other tribe is nearer... I can't stay present for long. Now they are all around me! I can see more closing in..."

Judith asked me to float out of my body. I heard her say, *"See the scene from above, Notice how you can view everything without being overwhelmed by it. You're safe, completely safe, floating above the pain and chaos. Try to observe your experience without judgment."*

Then she said, *"Notice the pain, the fear, the helplessness, but know you are safe here, in this space. You can watch the scene, understand it, but it does not have to define you."*

I felt myself lifting out of my body, floating above the scene, watching my detached body, and feeling separate and safe.

I tell Judith, "I am watching from above. I see myself, scared and alone. The other tribe thinks I'm dead and they are leaving me. Now I see myself dragging my wounded body under a bush where I can die in peace before they kill me. Then I black out."

Judith asked me to go to the next significant moment, counting again, *"one... two... three...click."*

"It's early morning. I am still lying under the bush. I scream! I see a clan of hyenas getting close."

Judith instructed me to float out of my body again, and from my safe place above, I watch as they attack me, pulling my wounded body to pieces and eating it as I lay there dying. Through the pain, all I can think about is my beloved Tembisa and Kagiso all alone without a protector. Will they ever be safe again? Who will train Kagiso to hunt, and who will bed Tembisa when I'm gone?

Slowly, Judith brought me out of the trance by first asking me to feel the fabric of the reclining chair, then the comforting softness of the wrap around my body, and then to hear the sounds around us. I felt myself back in her office, warmly wrapped in a comfortable chair.

Once I was fully back in the room, she asked me to relax again and asked my permission to remove the spear. I had no idea what she meant or what she could do, but then I felt her hands against my back, reaching for the spearhead embedded there.

"Let the pain leave your body," she said. *"Imagine a warm light replacing it, soothing and nourishing your wound. Feel your body healing from the inside out."*

As I felt her extracting it, I could feel the release of the pain, the healing energy flowing into me. The pain was still there, but it no longer felt powerful; it was just a part of my story.

My breathing had been ragged with the pain of the extraction, but gradually it slowed, and I felt more relaxed. The session ended with me returning to full awareness and a renewed sense of hope and clarity. I felt strangely calm and centered.

James reached over and took my hand, and concern and hope flickered alternately in his eyes. He asked, "How do you feel now?"

"It's... different. Like I saw things I hadn't really allowed myself to see before. The pain I felt was so real, but somehow, I also felt... a distance from it, like I could finally breathe."

James nodded quietly. "I can see it on your face. You're lighter now. It's almost like there is a weight taken off your shoulders."

Judith reminded me to keep a journal about my hypnotherapy sessions for us to discuss in our debriefing sessions. She asked me to, *"Write down what you experienced, what came up for you awake or in dreams, and how you felt about it. Sometimes, just putting it into words helps make sense of what your subconscious is telling you and increases healing."*

When I first wrote about my dreams after the session, they were still filled with pain and dread. I hated having to record my feelings, but they were with me all the time, even while I was working. I would be sitting at the desk in my office when I suddenly felt that I was drifting back to that painful scene. I could feel a lump in my throat, and I became aware of a rapid pulse in my neck.

During one of these lapses, I left out an entire paragraph in the legal brief I was composing, and my boss threatened to fire me if I didn't focus on my work. This would not be the first job I lost because of anxiety that kept returning and distracting me from the task at hand.

At our debriefing session, I sat with Judith and James in calm silence for a moment. Judith invited me to share my impressions of the hypnotherapy experience. *"What stood out most to you?"*

I responded that ever since the hypnotherapy session, I kept remembering how I felt seeing the clan of hyenas approaching me. I was powerless and afraid. I admitted that I was reluctant to come back for the next session because the dreams I was having were so intense. I didn't want to re-experience that fear again.

However, I explained that when I watched what was happening as I floated above myself, being out of my body meant I could see that the pain *wasn't* everything. There was more to me than just suffering. And as I spoke, I became aware of the deep love on James' face. For the first time, I realized that I had never really been alone.

He remarked, "It was intense, but I could see her calming down, almost as though this was her first real step towards healing her pain instead of just fighting it."

Over the following days, I felt a strange sense of peace, even when I remembered that awful scene. I was no longer seeing myself as a victim. I was beginning to realize that I'm not as helpless as I've always believed, but that I'm resilient and can survive a great deal!

In reviewing my notes, I had written, "I saw how I was trapped in that moment, but I also felt a spark of strength, like I could have fought back or escaped. I realize now that part of my pain was not just physical, but also emotional. I was holding onto feelings of helplessness and guilt. I couldn't save my family. I was useless as a father and husband. I kept cycling between wishing that I had saved them and acknowledging that I couldn't have... it wasn't my fault."

In our next psychotherapy session, Judith remarked that I appeared more grounded and open to the idea that relief might be possible. She said healing could involve me embracing my vulnerability without shame. I was encouraged when she added that my emotional clarity was emerging and that I seemed to be more hopeful about the future.

Throughout the subsequent therapy sessions, Judith and I noted recurring themes: My inner strength resurfaced during my episodes of remembering my traumatic experience. It was almost as though I was being reminded of my inner resilience. Now I had the ability to view my pain from a detached yet compassionate perspective, as I had during the hypnotherapy session.

Over the course of our work together, my journey was both profound and illuminating. The hypnotherapy sessions opened a door into my subconscious, revealing that the traumatic scene had become intertwined and almost synonymous with my physical pain. I also realized that I had a reservoir of resilience that I had never imagined was there. James and I were beginning to plan trips and adventures that we had never thought possible. My future was now filled with hope. We continued our psychotherapy with Judith as she guided us to integrate what we had experienced and learned into our daily lives and relationships.

Reader Takeaway

The initial hypnotherapy session with Natalie and James marked a meaningful breakthrough. Natalie's subconscious had begun to process what her conscious mind had long denied, her innocence, her feelings of powerlessness, and her innate resilience. The emotional insights gained from this deep exploration offered her new pathways toward healing, understanding, and acceptance.

There were some significant similarities to Charlotte's story (Chapter 1), but also some marked differences. Once Natalie's spearhead had been metaphorically removed, her path toward healing should have been clear. However, she still carried a depth of guilt about not saving her family, and feeling that had she been stronger, wiser, and faster, she might have saved them. Charlotte, on the other hand, was a young child who acknowledged that she had no control over the situation and found it far easier to let go of the painful memories. The age at which pivotal events occur can have a powerful effect on both the retention of memory and the facility to resolve grief and guilt (Felitti et al., 1998).

In Natalie's case, both Natalie and James were ready to integrate the insights they had gained into their waking life. They were prepared to carry with them tools that extended well beyond the therapy room. They were both committed to continuing their work in couples' psychotherapy, and Natalie was able to resolve her guilt as she understood more of her story. Their relationship continued to improve and was enriched by their shared insight.

James' support and understanding were invaluable to Natalie in her healing journey. His belief in her allowed her to see herself differently and ultimately to forgive herself. She now understood that her pain was not simply a physical ailment but an emotional story waiting to be told (Van der Kolk, 2014). This knowledge had a profound impact on her view of herself and was a major turning point for her and for her relationship with James. He no longer felt that he had to protect her but was able to expect and enjoy a full adult relationship with her.

Natalie's progress was reflected in observable shifts. Natalie and James reported fewer moments of despair, a more relaxed posture, and a renewed sense of hope. Her back pain had become less oppressive, and she found herself engaging more actively with her family and friends. Recurring themes surfaced: the importance of acknowledging her vulnerability, forgiving herself, and recognizing her inner resilience. In addition, she slowly became more focused at work and was able to keep her job.

Natalie's journey reminds us that beneath our wounds lies an innate strength waiting to emerge, a shining testament to human resilience and the profound power of compassionate healing that resides within each of us, waiting to be awakened. The chronic pain became a metaphor for unaddressed grief and unspoken trauma (Pohl, 2012).

The emotional significance of the memory of her grandmother's garden became clearer: it was her childhood innocence, her connection to nature, and her sense of belonging. As our work progressed, this 'Place of Joy' helped her reconnect with her innate strength and positivity, providing a foundation for the transformative work ahead. It became not just a memory, but a symbol of resilience, reminding her that peace and healing are always within reach.

Chronic pain based on physical injury and other underlying physical problems can also be increased and become unbearable when accompanied by emotional pain that has not been acknowledged (Pohl & Ketcham, 2015). When families are stoic and only physical pain can be expressed or attended to, emotional pain can transform into physical pain or be attached to real physical pain.

Natalie's pain was based on a past life physical injury that had carried through to her present life and served her well as an expression of need that her family could acknowledge. Only the physical pain was recognized as something that might need outside intervention. However, it also created barriers to her expressing emotional vulnerability or seeking help for emotional distress. In both instances, past life regression hypnotherapy can be extremely helpful.[1]

Note

1 There is a wealth of research and literature on the many methods that are effective for managing chronic emotional and physical pain. The most notable work is that of Van der Kolk (2014). Other approaches include the polyvagal method (Porges, 2011; Pohl, 2012; Pohl & Ketcham, 2015); neurofeedback (Roy et al., 2020); eye movement desensitization and reprocessing [EMDR] (Shapiro, 2018); cognitive behavior therapy [CBT] (Beck, 1979), (Otis et al., 2021); and varying combinations of psychotherapy, both individual (Leong et al., 2023) and family (Minuchin & Fishman, 1981; Schwartz, 1995), as well as physical and occupational therapy and pharmacological interventions. Past Life Regression Hypnotherapy is a useful addition to our toolset for managing emotional, psychological, and physical pain (Burgess, 2020; Weiss, 1988).

Chapter 3

Will I See You Again?

Sometimes, in the half-light between waking and memory,
I feel you brush past me,
a reminder that love does not end,
it only changes its distance.

Author

Carl and his family came to the first appointment overwhelmed with grief at the loss of Carl's wife, Jennifer. Through hypnotherapy, they hoped to make sense of her untimely death. At the appointment were: Carl (Jennifer's husband); Felicia (Jennifer's mother), and Carl and Jennifer's two children, Teddy (14) and Karen (16). They were all hoping to find answers to their unresolved questions and to seek help for dealing with this catastrophic loss.

Carl's Story

I don't know how I arrived at Judith's office that first day without collapsing under the weight of it all. I'd been living in a fog since the night I found Jennifer's lifeless body on the floor with empty prescription bottles nearby. She had no pulse, no breath, no heartbeat, nothing. I tried CPR, prayed, begged, screamed. The paramedics came, and all the way through the ambulance ride, I prayed. But at the hospital, they pronounced her dead. I stood there, unable to believe that my wife, the woman who filled every corner of my life, was gone.

Since that night, everything had been a blur. My mother-in-law, Felicia, stepped in to care for our children, Teddy aged 14 and Karen aged 16, while I stumbled through the days unable to be there for my children. I was drowning in guilt, not only from her death but also from everything that came before it.

DOI: 10.4324/9781003636182-4

I was relieved that my family could come with me to my first session with Judith. They were hurting as much as I was, and I hoped that she could help us all. I told Judith that for many years, Jennifer had suffered terrible neck pain from degenerative spinal discs. Nothing relieved her constant pain. She was stoic, but I knew it was excruciating and I felt helpless as she struggled with pain every day.

For quite a while, Jennifer had tried not to drink or take any medication, but before her death, she began taking painkillers, and we both started drinking too much. I knew I needed to stop drinking, but I rationalized that I didn't want her drinking alone. So, I kept her company. I knew that she was also taking as much oxycodone as she could find. At least I resisted those. I just couldn't share with anyone else how worried I was about her.

I watched helplessly as the pain wore her down until even living felt like what she described as "an unbearable weight." Despite the pills and the alcohol, the pain never left her. As I explained to Judith, I wanted to be supportive, so most nights I joined her and we both numbed ourselves with whatever we had available. I told myself that for me, drinking with her was easier than watching helplessly from the sidelines. However, whether I wanted to admit it or not, the uncomfortable fact was that I was no longer 'in recovery' from alcoholism (Stanton & Todd, 1982). I convinced myself that people would understand my relapse, and no one could fault me for it.

Telling Judith all of this felt overwhelming. I told her about our life together, my beloved Jennifer and me. We loved to travel. We went on a cruise just before she died. We had planned this cruise as the beginning of a special time together. However, she was in so much pain that she couldn't even leave the cabin to explore the ship. I wanted to do something to help her but had no idea what I could do. I begged her to see the ship's doctor. All he did was give her more pain pills. This was just like her own doctor, who had told us that there was nothing that could be done to alleviate her pain. The situation seemed hopeless to Jennifer, and despite the constant reality, I always believed that we would find some way to get help. Jennifer killed herself a month after our cruise.

As I told Judith about it, Felicia (Jennifer's mother) sat beside our children, Teddy and Karen, with one hand resting on each of their knees. They were all crying softly. I could barely keep talking. It hurt too much. Jennifer had not only been brave, but she was also wise and conscientious. After her death, I learned that she'd even taken the time to put her affairs in order. She also left me a letter thanking me for our life together and telling me she loved me. Reading it was almost harder than losing her.

After her death, it was as though she had never really left. I still felt her presence everywhere. One day, her favorite perfume bottle fell from the bathroom shelf and shattered. No one was near it at the time. It was the bottle I had given her for her last birthday, knowing how much she loved the fragrance. Her morning bird would whistle outside our window at dawn, just at the time that she used to feed him. Sometimes I saw her face in the clouds. Friends told me they had seen her shadow in the garden. She was here, my guardian angel, still helping me. She's even guided me back to regular meditation and the church. I know she wanted me to be healthy and to feel whole. I also knew that my sobriety meant a great deal to her.

Felicia told me she too believed that Jennifer was still present. She said Jennifer came to her in the form of a hawk that circled her yard. One day, she said that the hawk brought her a silent message: *"Had you known the suffering that was yet to come, you would not have wanted me to continue living."* Felicia continued, "The words sounded exactly like my daughter, always selfless, always protecting us."

Still, despite everyone else's reassurance and my feeling that her spirit was still nearby, my wife was gone, and I couldn't stop feeling guilty. I kept thinking: *What if I'd seen the signs? What if I'd stopped her?* I asked Judith, "What would have happened if I had stayed sober? Was I wrong to keep her company with the drinking?"

I told Judith that I knew how much my sobriety meant to Jennifer, but I convinced myself that my drinking with her was my way of being supportive. My guilt, my doubts, and my loneliness brought up so many questions. Was I trying to avoid the guilt I felt about relapsing after 16 years of sobriety? Would she have taken her life if I'd been more present for her or understood her pain? Will I ever find peace again now that my dearest one is gone? I came to Judith along with my family because I was overwhelmed with emotional pain, and I wasn't sure how to live with it.

After hearing my story, Judith had several suggestions about good ways to start our work together. One was that I explore the wonder and joy of our relationship. This might help illuminate how special our love had been. She explained that the reason I was feeling such intense grief was because of the deep bond we had with each other. She suggested our sharing her favorite books and music and looking through old photographs together, and that going forward, I should remember that what we had shared was unique and irreplaceable, and this special relationship would never be lost.

Judith wanted all of us to attend 12-step or other fellowship meetings. She offered to provide me with additional treatment resources for my grief and alcohol issues, should I need them. This was important because Judith explained how catastrophic loss can precipitate relapse (Garrett & Landau, 2007).[1] My family and friends had been worried about our/my drinking, and they all committed to attending meetings to support my journey back into sobriety. They were relieved that there was something they could do to help me with my unresolved grief.

Judith explained to the family that she would like to start working with me alone, saying, "*Maybe some of the answers lie in who you were together before this lifetime, or who you'll be together in the future.*"

She told the family that they could participate in future sessions to explore their past relationships with our beloved Jennifer. My family seemed relieved that my distress would be addressed first.

Feeling well prepared, I was excited to begin my Past Life Regression Hypnotherapy journey. My first past life hypnotherapy journey started with Judith guiding me to discover my 'Place of Joy.' She told me that she worked with a very light hypnotic state and that I would be able to talk freely with her and have perfect recall of the entire session.

She said, "*Together, you and I will explore who you have been in your past, where you have traveled, and try to find solace through the experience. We will explore how you and Jennifer have been together in one or more lifetimes.*"

Judith suggested that Jennifer had chosen to leave me at a time when I could still feel some of the joy of her presence, rather than only the misery of her pain. Judith explained that Jennifer was still deeply in love with me. That is why she continued to take care of me as best she could through her spiritual messages. Although it is apparently very hard for spirits to move objects, she managed to do it to show me that she was still connected with me.

I told Judith how much Jennifer and I loved traveling together, whether in the car, on a cruise, or on a train. Just being together meant everything to us. "I've been trying to recreate our trips together, challenging myself to repeat the journeys thinking it might help me find my lost happiness." I asked Judith whether she could help me rediscover the joy, rather than my life being filled with pain.

Judith began the hypnotherapy session with the progressive relaxation exercise that I had been practicing since the previous session. Once I was ready and relaxed, I stretched out on the recliner, snuggled into a warm wrap, and began to let go completely as she counted down from 10 to 1. I followed her instruction to go to the joy and bliss of my relationship with Jennifer and to avoid the ongoing misery of her pain.

She invited me to select a pathway into this journey of exploration as I found my 'Place of Joy.' I was offered several induction options: walking down a garden path, floating on top of clear water in a pond, or burrowing far down into the depths of the earth. I chose to wander down a garden path. Then Judith asked me, "*What do you hear, see, smell or feel?*"

"I feel the air cool against my skin, smell the grass, and hear the quiet trickle of a stream nearby."

Judith's voice guided me gently: *"Go to a place in the past where you felt joy and love with Jennifer."* I followed her voice as she told me to travel back to a time of meaning. I felt myself relax for the first time in months.

When she counted, *"one...two...three,"* and clicked her fingers, I saw an old wooden gate with a rusty latch. It opened easily, and I walked through it into the sunlight. Again, I heard the soft murmur of water nearby. Everything was peaceful. I had found my 'Place of Joy.'

Judith reminded me that this would be my safe space, my place to go to when I met a stressful situation in real life or during hypnotherapy. She had me spend a little time enjoying the peace and comfort of this sacred place.

When I was ready, Judith asked me to move backward in time to a moment of significance with Jennifer, *"one...two...three.... click. What can you see, hear, feel, sense, and smell?"*

I remember my joy. I was back with Jennifer on our first date and feeling wonderfully happy. It was a clear spring day and she was excited. She looked stunning! I was sitting at one end of the table and she at the other. I was thinking how I really liked this woman. She seemed so smart. I must get to know her.

Judith asked me to move further back in time. *"One... two... three... click..."* "It's 1929.

There's a farm way in the distance. I can see a beautiful meadow and a big valley. Jennifer is there in the distance with my sister. She's wearing a red and white checkered shirt and pants. She's young and very pretty and she is looking right at me. We are both so happy."

"Go to the next significant moment. "One... two... three... click..."

"We're walking towards the farm and there is a big barn. There's a horse in the barn. Oh! It's her horse. She really loves that horse. Jennifer is so lovely, tall and slender."

"One... two... three... click..." "She's on her horse riding around the corral. I'm walking over to be closer to her. She is 22 and I'm 23. A dog is running under the fence. Her horse is spooked. I can't get to her. The horse is rearing up... she's hanging on! I'm screaming, 'Don't let go!!!' I am so scared, she's in the air... falling! She's hit the back of her head on the fence... I can't watch!"

I was panicking. Judith asked me to float up to a place of emotional safety where I could watch what was happening while I could protect myself from intense feelings. She said that if I couldn't do that, I could return to my 'Place of Joy.'

I felt myself rising out of my body and watching what was happening below me.

"One, two, three, click..." Judith asked me, *"What is happening? What do you see, feel, smell, hear?"*

"As I watch from above, I see myself running to pick Jennifer up. I can't stay away. I'm holding her in my arms, crying, and rocking her. I know that she's already dead, but I must revive her. She isn't moving or breathing. I'm confused and running about with her in my arms. Some men are trying to take her away from me. Where are they going? Where are they taking her? I'm trying to stop them! I don't know what to do! I'm in shock. I can't move. I'm sobbing and my fists are clenched. I can't breathe."

At that point, Judith brought me out of my hypnotic state, and after a warm cup of herbal tea and some soothing, I was able to stop sobbing and be fully present. We talked briefly and she sent me to her beautiful garden where I could sit quietly, relax, and calm down before driving home.

It took me a good half hour to settle down and feel that I was truly back in the present and ready to tackle the traffic! My experience stayed with me until we met for our next session, where we planned to compare and combine her notes with my experience during and after the first session.

During our next session, Judith and I reviewed her first session notes along with mine. I also told her about my experiences both when awake and while dreaming. I felt that the debriefing validated my experiences and gave me a new and more objective perspective.

Then we reviewed all that I had written in my journal. "I've been feeling helpless all over again, just like when I was trying to save her after her horse threw her. I couldn't save her then. I can't save her now. I have never felt this deep sense of shock and loss before. I don't know what to do with it."

Judith quietly reassured me, saying, *"Sometimes our only option is to come to terms with our loss. This is the opportunity that Jennifer has given you. She is offering you a chance to save a perfect relationship rather than carrying another horrific loss."*

Judith helped me understand that Jennifer was trying to save me from the suffering I had gone through with her before. I began to realize that she was leaving me with beautiful memories of our most recent time together, hoping to heal the past rather than repeating and increasing my pain.

How beautiful she was both now and then. I wished I could have sat with her body and closed her eyelids and heard her say that she would wait for me until the end of time. I didn't know then, but I knew now that she did! I felt better about saying goodbye this time, and I think I was beginning to understand that she died now for both of us. But I still wished that she'd had time to say goodbye.

I asked Judith whether Jennifer thought I wouldn't support her leaving? That I couldn't handle it? I paused and thought about it. Jennifer was right. She chose the only way to spare me the pain of the last time!

As Judith had suggested, I shared the story with my family before they came with me to our next meeting. They were all eager to rediscover their beloved daughter and mother. At our initial session, Judith had asked the family to practice progressive relaxation and to be ready to join me wherever I took them. I reminded them that we would be in a light state of hypnosis and reassured them again that if the situation became too much to bear, Judith would guide them to a safe, protected place as she had with me.

We all began the family hypnotherapy session with progressive relaxation, and Judith asked how we would like to get to a peaceful 'Place of Joy' prior to entering the journey into our shared past. She explained that we did not need to share a place, but that we could share it if we chose to do so.

We all chose to be together on this journey and selected a place that we all loved. It was next to a lake where we had enjoyed camping as a family with Jennifer. Judith explained again that the 'Place of Joy' was a sacred space to which any of us could return as needed during the hypnotherapy sessions.

Judith explained how she counts and that we might find ourselves together, or apart. Whichever happened, it would be what we needed. I described how I had wandered down a garden path to the old wooden gate and the family agreed to do the same.

The instruction to all of us was, "*Go to a place in an earlier lifetime when you, Jennifer, Felicia and the children were all together.*" Judith counted down from 10 to 1, then clicked her fingers, asking us, "*What do you hear, see, sense, smell or feel?*"

I returned to a light hypnotic state very quickly. I believe that everyone in the family was relaxed, and later they said that they all felt as though they were in a light trance and participating with me.

I'm alone in a sage brush arbor. There's nobody around. I think I'm in the west somewhere. It's 1878. It's a small Western town. There aren't any people. I think it may be a ghost town. I just keep walking. The street is very dusty. My old shoes are grey. I don't know where to go. There's a train stopping. I'm getting on. I think the other people sitting with me are a family. Maybe they're going further west. I've no idea where I'm going.

Suddenly, I recognize the mother of the family. It's my beloved Jennifer. She looks very different. I just sit quietly, waiting to see what happens next.

A young girl sitting across from me in the carriage suddenly blurts out, "I'm on the train." I recognize her as a much younger Felicia (my mother-in-law).

She continues, "Grandma died just before we left." I realize that she is referring to her grandmother, Jennifer's great-grandmother.

She says, "I'm sad that she isn't with us anymore. My mother has the baby." I wondered what baby?

Judith said, "*Go to the next significant moment together...one...two...three...click.*"

Judith asked Felicia, "*Please look at your feet and then let your eyes travel up your body, all the way to your face and tell me your name and how old you are.*"

Felicia answered, "I'm wearing button boots and a smock. I just turned 8. I haven't had a party because we're on the train. Mother promised we could have a party when we got there."

Judith repeated her question, "*Your name?*"

She replied, "Dorothy. Father says that I'm a big girl now and need to help him because Grandma died, and Mother is weak from the baby."

Judith then asked Felicia, "*Dorothy, who is with you on the train? Do you recognize them from your current lifetime?*"

She replied, "I think that Jennifer is my mother, and the baby is my granddaughter, Karen."

I realized that my Jennifer had originally been Felicia's mother in the lifetime we were visiting together. The baby she was caring for was our daughter Karen.

Dorothy talked about their plans to move West and how they'd been exhausted by the journey. They had to stay awake to protect their belongings from the thieves who frequently board West-bound trains and stagecoaches.

I started crying quietly and Judith asked me, "*Carl, what's making you sad?*"

I answered that I knew what happens next. "I'd had nightmares about it, but I didn't know it was real and from my past. This was the first time I lost Jennifer: She was the mother of Dorothy (Felicia)!"

"A man has just burst into our compartment! He's waving his gun at me and demanding that we all give him our food and money. I try to tell him that we wouldn't survive! He says he'll kill us all! He lifts and aims the shotgun at me. I feel a hard punch in my chest."

Judith asked me, "*Carl, please float out of your body to the space above where you can see and hear everything but feel no pain. Are you there?*"

"Yes! He's attacking and undressing Dorothy's mother, Jennifer, and the children are crying. I can't move. I can't do anything! I'm just lying on the floor, bleeding while he violates Jennifer and kills Dorothy (Felicia) and everyone else in the compartment."

During my journaling and subsequent debriefing session, I realized that I have had many romantic relationships, attempting to end my solitude. I've spent a lifetime trying to find the perfect love to fill my "soul loneliness." Jennifer was the only one who had ever truly shared that space. She never forgot a birthday or any of our special events. She also reminded all the others in the family about special occasions.

She was my role model, and I needed to learn how to be without her in this lifetime. She would want me to continue for the sake of our family. I can't imagine ever being ready for another romantic relationship, but I'm no longer worried about being destined to be alone. I've been with my one true love and believe we will meet again.

Reader Takeaway

Unlike Chapters 1 and 2, where the primary reason for referral was the person with the presenting problem,[2] in this chapter, the entire family is grieving and involved in the process of searching for relief (Garrett & Landau, 2007).

During debriefing, once Carl had shared his new insight about Jennifer's choosing suicide, Felicia talked about her own nightmares and her reluctance to travel by train. She explained how she had worried about leaving Jennifer alone when she was a young child. As a result, Jennifer had developed anxiety about going to nursery school, and they needed family therapy to address her 'separation anxiety' (Benoit, 2004).

Felicia now understood that it was based on her earlier lifetime loss. Felicia was grateful for understanding where the issue had originated and felt that this experience would also help her grieve for her daughter in a healthier way. She realized that she should be a little less protective of her grandchildren now that she understood the origin of her separation anxiety.

After the work together, the entire family felt they understood Jennifer's premature death and were able to forgive her for leaving them. Even though cognitively they knew that Jennifer was no longer present, the entire family had trouble with grieving and moving on. They all felt what they described as the constant presence of Jennifer.

Being introduced to Pauline Boss's (2006) concept of ambiguous loss, they were able to understand their experiences. The family also felt reassured that since their souls had been together in the past, they would be together again in the future.

In Chapters 1 and 2, the healing occurred for the 'person of concern,' which helped the families deal with their loved one. In this instance, like Ahmad in Chapter 5 and Ana in Chapter 6, the entire family was involved throughout and was able to heal as a group.

Sometimes those intergenerational patterns do not originate in this lifetime but come from earlier periods when we were together in other lifetimes. Adding Past Life Regression Hypnotherapy to one's choices of therapy can provide astonishing insights and guide the therapy journey to resolution in unexpected ways. Experiences like this are universal (Walsh & McGoldrick, 1991). Once we understand the past, we can explain and resolve present challenges moving forward into the future with hope and trust (Landau, 2018).

It was extremely helpful for the family to revisit the strengths of their ancestors and past lives, rather than dwelling on their vulnerability. By recognizing the strength of their relationships and love for one another, they were able to face the present, determined to bring their past resilience and survivor skills into their future.

Notes

1 YouTube video by Judith Landau, "Family Stories, Secrets, and Survival," January 25, 2013.
2 Person of Concern, or POC, is the term used to denote the person with the presenting problem.

Chapter 4

Are We Meant to Be Together?

I walked a path made of starlight, certain I would find you there.
Even in the quiet between worlds, your presence shimmered,
a warmth I recognized before I remembered your face.

Author

Pauline and Malcolm, a middle-aged professional couple, both in their second marriage, were intrigued to explore the meaning of their relationship. *Why did we recognize each other on our first meeting? Why the intensity of familiarity? Have we been together before? Will we be together again?*

They elected to experience their Past Life Regression Hypnotherapy together. The process began with each of their individual journeys (while the other observed in silence). They processed both individual sessions together, and we then did a joint regression. The couple found themselves reuniting in several past lifetimes. They felt the magic of recognition and the realization that yes, they were meant to be together in this lifetime as well.

Pauline's Story

I still remember the first time I saw Malcolm. It was at a conference neither of us had planned to attend. I felt it before I even spoke to him, a sudden warmth in my chest, a flutter that made my hands clammy. And when he looked at me, I could see it in his eyes as well: a flicker of something unspoken, something that felt like recognition. We both knew, in that strange, inexplicable way, that something had shifted. Not slowly, not gradually, but instantly. Have we met before? Or is this… fate?

Malcolm's life, like mine, was complicated. We were both leaving our first marriages, carrying histories and children and homes already full of love and loss. And yet, that first glance made me question everything

DOI: 10.4324/9781003636182-5

I thought I knew about timing, love, and destiny. I noticed the way he hesitated before he laughed, the subtle tension in his shoulders that hinted at past hurts, the way his gaze lingered just long enough to feel like an invitation. In that moment, all the noise of our lives fell away.

When we sat down with Judith, we weren't broken. We both told her that we weren't seeking to fix anything. We wanted to understand why the connection between us felt so timeless, so undeniable.

"I just need to know this isn't fleeting," I admitted quietly. My voice felt small in the room, vulnerable in a way I rarely allowed myself.

Malcolm reached over and brushed my hand with his. "I feel the same. It's like... we've been looking for each other without knowing it. We would love to explore our past lives and find out whether and where we have been together."

His words were slow and deliberate, but they carried a weight that I felt in my bones.

We told Judith what we hoped for, not marriage, not a new beginning in the usual sense, but a bond strong enough to support all our children, our families, and each other. We wanted to deepen what was already there. Beneath our words, I think we both hoped for reassurance: that this wasn't just chemistry, but something larger, enduring, maybe even eternal.

I found myself noticing how intently Malcolm listened and his expression as he seemed to relate to something tender or painful. It was as if every gesture, no matter how small, confirmed that ours was more than a chance encounter.

Judith asked us about our 'Places of Joy,' moments or places that brought us each deep peace.

I expected Malcolm to say a favorite hike or a song he loved. But he looked at me and said softly, "It's when I look at you and know you."

I realized mine was the same. My joy wasn't in a place, it was in him, in the instant recognition that had pulled us together. That became our anchor. Whenever we closed our eyes in therapy, whenever we tried to calm ourselves in moments of uncertainty, that spark, the click of belonging, was always there.

The room smelled faintly of lavender. Reclining in comfortable chairs, with a soft wrap over my knees, I felt his hand briefly brush mine, grounding me. Judith's voice guided us down a path of stillness and relaxation. She asked us if we wanted to picture ourselves on a sunny, quiet beach, a shaded forest, a beautiful garden, or a completely different place that we loved. We chose our favorite camping ground next to a quiet stream.

She took us through progressive relaxation that we had practiced at home to be prepared for our first hypnotherapy session. We were ready.

Judith counted very slowly and softly from 1 to 10 while asking us to close our eyes, relax completely, and feel our eyes and limbs getting heavier and heavier. She asked us to return to a place where we had been together at a significant time.

At first, it was nothing but quiet. And then… images began to appear.

Judith asked, *"Where are you? What are you wearing? How old are you? What year is it? What do you see, hear, smell, touch?"*

"I'm on a cobblestone street in France, a basket of bread in my arms. It's 1753. Across the way, a man in rough wool stops. I know him. His eyes locked with mine, and a rush of recognition fills me.

"Malcolm…" I breathe, my voice catching. "It's the same for me," he whispers back. "I am there. I recognize you."

Judith asked us to go to the next significant moment. She counted, *"1…2…3…click"*

The scene shifts to a desert. Heat presses down on my shoulders, and my hands are rough from carrying water. A caravan appears, and a thirsty rider approaches. It is he. Our hands brush as I pass him a jar of water, and sparks leap between us. I notice a surge of gratitude, as if the smallest acts of kindness could echo across centuries.

"Go to the next significant moment where the two of you are together, "1…2…3…click"

I'm in a lush green valley surrounded by hills. I realize I am in England. I'm dressed in a blue peasant skirt with a puffy white blouse and a white apron. I see a young man in farm clothes coming down the hill with his sheepdog.

He sees me, and I see him. 'I recognize this beautiful girl,' he says aloud, almost laughing. "It is she." I feel laughter bubble up inside me too, a pure, untethered delight.

Judith brought us out of our trance counting backward from 10 to 1, and we slowly came back into the room, feeling the chair, listening to the sounds around us, and smelling the soft lavender-scented air.

When the session ended, we opened our eyes and held each other's gaze. Tears streaked my face. There was a tenderness in that room, a quiet reverence that neither of us had anticipated. It was as if the universe had finally paused to let us see ourselves fully. We both felt relaxed and ready to go home together. Judith reminded both of us to journal our experience of the session and whatever memories arose before the next meeting with her.

"That… doesn't change anything, does it?" I whispered to him that night in bed. "No," he responded softly, shaking his head. "It explains everything."

We returned the next day with our journals in hand. I had written down every detail I could remember: the textures, the smells, the way my body had responded. Malcolm's journal was equally full.

Judith asked, *"What did you notice when you wrote about the experience?"*

I flipped through my pages. "It's the small gestures… the recognition in his eyes, the instinctive connection before any words were spoken. I didn't realize my body remembered before my mind did."

Malcolm added, "I noticed my emotions, joy and fear at the same time. Writing it down made me see how deeply connected it felt."

Judith said, *"These reflections help you integrate your experiences between sessions. They make the feelings more tangible and anchored in your present lives."*

Between sessions, I found myself noticing Malcolm in ordinary moments; how he paused to really listen, how his attention lingered in small, affirming ways. Writing about it made these subtle recognitions feel more alive. I also found myself remembering more about the hypnotherapy session, and I was able to relate to Judith's description of our experience from her own notes.

We had two more sessions. Each time, our stories overlapped like threads in the same tapestry. We were children running barefoot through fields, elders holding hands in small villages, soldiers, healers, lovers, and rivals. Centuries ago, we had raised twin boys together, only to lose them. Through every lifetime, through every loss and joy, we had always found each other.

After each session, I felt calmer, steadier, more certain. Malcolm felt it too. It wasn't just about knowing the past, it was about recognizing a truth that lived in the present: our bond, our connection, our love, had roots deeper than any one lifetime could contain. In those sessions, I became aware of the textures of our shared histories… the scent of sea air on long-forgotten beaches, the way his hand fit in mine in countless forms, the quiet humor we shared even in hardship and grief. It was not just memory; it was a feeling embedded in my very being.

The following weeks brought subtle changes that surprised us both. Malcolm remarked, "I noticed that Pauline was calmer, more patient with our children." I noticed Malcolm's small gestures of tenderness more, and he noticed mine. We didn't need constant reassurance anymore; the recognition we had witnessed in our shared pasts had become a quiet, unwavering trust in each other.

We began talking about sharing some of our stories with our children, in small, careful ways. We wanted them to understand that love can exist across time, generations, and circumstances. These conversations were delicate, filled with pauses, laughter, and wonder.

Our children noticed the warmth, the patience, and the way we seemed to move in harmony, as if guided by an invisible current. We felt our wonderful extended and blended family coming together more closely and with a new understanding of what had led us to be together again.

Reader Takeaway

Pauline and Malcolm's story shows that love doesn't always require mending a wound. Sometimes, it's about affirming wholeness, honoring recognition, and building trust. Whether or not you believe in past lives, the experience of recognizing someone as deeply connected to you, across time, memory, or metaphor, can transform how you relate to them and to your combined extended family (Burgess, 2020; Weiss, 1996; Woolger, 1988).

For this couple, love had continuity, and through that recognition, they found peace, clarity, and a shared joy that they hadn't known was missing. They began to realize that in every glance, in every shared silence, their connection was more than circumstance. It was a thread woven across time, fragile yet enduring, visible only to those who recognize it. The reader will understand that our important relationships have meaning not only in the here and now, but also through time.

Chapter 5

From Trauma to Resilience

I have walked through the dark with only my breath for company,
but even there, a seed of light waited for me.
When I finally reached it,
I realized it had been growing inside me all along.

Author

Refugee Iranian parents, Leila and Aziz, requested help for their 16-year-old son, Ahmad, who was having trouble at school because of his bad behavior and substance use. His grades had dropped dramatically. His parents suspected that he was using street drugs and felt that his school friends' influence was driving him away from them and into secrecy.

Leila, Aziz, Ahmad, and his younger brother Masoud (aged 14) shared one room while the rest of the extended family shared the other two rooms. All 13 family members had escaped persecution and possible imprisonment or death in Iran. Ahmad had become distant from his parents after his transition to middle school. This coincided with an additional aunt, uncle, and three cousins (one his age) moving into their already overcrowded space.

Everyone old enough to work had at least one job. Despite being highly qualified in their own country of origin, none of those qualifications was recognized in their new home. Each of the adults was dealing with feelings of failure and despair, leading to numerous petty arguments and disharmony (Landau, 1982).

Family members were reluctant to talk about anything intimate and avoided sharing any traumatic memories. With the entire family being involved in the original trauma, it would be essential to involve them in all aspects of the therapy process (Falicov, 2012). After several extended family sessions, we began Past Life Regression Hypnotherapy (PLRH) with Aziz, Leila, their children Ahmad and Masoud, and maternal grandmother, Ariana.

DOI: 10.4324/9781003636182-6

Ahmad's Story Several Years After His Hypnotherapy Work

I didn't want anyone to know how lonely I felt. At home, there were ten of us crammed into two rooms. Every night, people came home exhausted, while others left for work. The air was thick with smoke and the clatter of dishes. The squeak of worn floorboards made sleep almost impossible. The sounds of arguments and chores, shouting and laughter blended into an indecipherable hum that never stopped. I felt like I had to shrink myself just to survive, curl into a corner, breathe quietly, make myself invisible.

At school, it was different. With my friends, the misfits, the ones who skipped class, smoked, and made noise, I finally felt seen. Even if some of them were bullies, at least I existed in their eyes. When I first tried pot with them, it helped me sleep through the chaos at home. It dulled my fear, even if only for a little while. I hated that I needed it, but it was the first time I could breathe, and with my friends, I could feel my chest expand, my shoulders relax, my racing thoughts slow for a moment.

After seeing a therapist for a few unsuccessful sessions, my parents persuaded me to have a consultation with Judith, a psychiatrist and hypnotherapist who had worked successfully with the son of one of their friends. They wanted me to try PLRH as a last resort.

When I first came to see Judith with my parents, Leila and Aziz, my grandmother, Ariana, and my younger brother (Masoud), I didn't really want to be there. But something told me I had to try. I squared my shoulders, took a deep breath, and decided that whatever happened couldn't be more chaotic or painful than what was currently occurring.

Judith asked me to describe a space where I felt safety and peace. She explained that during our work together, that place would become my 'Place of Joy.'

I thought for a moment, then drifted to the backyard of my childhood under the old maple tree. The grass smelled sweet after the rain, and the bark pressed roughly against my back. The sun dappled my face, warm and tender. Our dog lay beside me, breathing slowly, the soft rhythm of his body grounding me. Here, I didn't have to be scared. No one demanded anything of me. I could just exist. That was joy.

My mother's eyes glistened when she shared that her 'Place of Joy' was shelling peas with her grandmother on the porch. She said, "I can almost hear the snap of pods and smell the lingering green scent on my fingers."

My grandmother, Ariana, remembered her childhood kitchen, the scent of simmering soup, the rhythmic clink of a wooden spoon against a pot. Even my father and Masoud, my younger brother, found quiet, secret places where they felt anchored; my father in his workshop, inhaling the scent of sawdust and oil, and Masoud beneath a streetlamp, staring up at stars in silence.

The first hypnotherapy session was overwhelming. The room felt heavy, my body tight. Judith dimmed the lights and led me through what she called progressive relaxation. I felt each muscle tighten then loosen; shoulders dropping, jaw unclenching.

Once Judith felt I was completely relaxed, she asked me to feel myself sinking into the reclining chair, letting myself feel heavy, and feeling my eyelids closing. She counted from 1 to 10 and asked me on the count of 10 to imagine moving to a significant time in the past when I was with my family.

I wasn't in Judith's office anymore. I was in a palace. Golden light poured through high windows, fountains glittered, and the scent of roses filled the air. I wore silk robes, and even my parents bowed to me. My brother looked at me for guidance. I was strong and powerful, and I felt like I belonged.

Then Judith's voice intruded, *"Go to the next significant moment, 1...2...3...click."*

Suddenly, everything shifted. I was younger and I was caught in a terrible choice: Join the enemy with their atrocities or watch my family die. I was frozen, terrified, and seeing horrible things happen that I didn't want to see.

Judith asked me to float above it all. From high above, I could see what was happening without feeling the fear. My mother's tears glistened in the dim light, my father's hands shook, and my brother reached out toward me. I could see them all, but I wasn't overwhelmed.

Judith's voice reminded me, *"You are not powerless now. You are here with your family. Feel their presence, their caring. You're no longer alone."*

When I came out of my trance, I whispered something I had kept hidden: "I didn't want to tell you how lonely I was. I didn't want to worry you anymore."

My father reached across the chair, placing his hand over mine, "We are stronger together. Don't shut us out."

My mother brushed a stray hair from my face, her fingers lingering on my cheek, "We were so focused on survival, we forgot how you were hurting. Please forgive us."

My grandmother's voice was soft, almost a sigh, "The silence is broken. We remember our roots, and we remember our courage."

In the next session, our whole family was hypnotized again, and we all returned to our 'Places of Joy.' I saw the maple tree again, leaves whispering secrets just for me, my dog curled at my side. I felt lighter, a weight lifted from my chest.

My mother, who in previous family sessions had been in her own 'Place of Joy,' followed me into mine. She seemed afraid, but I whispered to her, "It's okay. You're not alone. We are all here together."

In that moment, something shifted in all of us. This session had not provided any dramatic revelation, but we were together, safe in each other's presence, and it felt very good.

At our next session, Judith dimmed the lights again, the amber glow wrapping the room in warmth. A faint scent of lavender drifted from a diffuser, mingling with the quiet hum of the air conditioner. I sank into the chair, my body heavy, yet ready.

"Close your eyes," Judith said, her voice soft but firm. *"Take a deep breath. Imagine stepping back in time to meet the younger you. Not to relive the fear, but to comfort him."*

I felt the familiar pull, like sinking into a pool of memory. The air shimmered, and suddenly, I was ten years old again. I was curled under the thin blanket in our cramped room, clutching it around my shoulders. Smoke lingered in the air, and the distant shouts of adults echoed through the walls. My heart thudded, fast and erratic. Then I saw him (me), wide-eyed, trembling, lips pressed together to keep quiet.

Judith's voice floated to me: *"Step closer. What does he need to hear?"*

I swallowed hard. My throat felt tight. "You're safe now," I whispered. "You're not alone. We will be okay."

The younger me blinked, body stiff. I reached out slowly, and he hesitated before allowing me to pull him into an embrace. His tiny arms clung to me, and for the first time, I felt the raw weight of all those years of fear, loneliness, and silence.

Tears pooled in my eyes. "I've carried this too long," I admitted to him. "But it's not yours to carry anymore. It's ours, together."

Judith counted from 1 to 5 and instructed us to move to the next significant moment together.

The younger versions of my mother, father, Ariana, and Masoud appeared beside us. My mother knelt next to her younger self, brushing a strand of hair from her forehead. "I'm here now," she whispered. "I see you. I feel you. I'm sorry we weren't always strong enough before."

My grandmother's voice trembled beside me: "I'm scared..." I reached for her hand, holding it tight. "It's okay. You're not alone. We're here."

Even my father knelt by his childhood self, the tension in his shoulders easing. And my grandmother, usually silent and composed, allowed a faint smile as she hugged her younger version, their hands clasped like a lifeline.

Judith's voice guided us further: *"Now, let your younger selves imagine a garden. Feel the sunlight, hear the birds, smell the flowers. Sit together, past and present, and let the fear dissolve into safety."*

Our garden was breathtaking. Sunlight streamed through leafy branches, casting dancing shadows on the soft grass. A gentle breeze carried the scent of jasmine and lavender. Birds sang above, and there was only laughter, quiet at first, then full and free.

I watched as my family, the little children we once were and the older people we had become, sit together in a circle. The younger me leaned against me, sighing in relief. My mother laughed softly, her eyes bright. Grandmother's shoulders relaxed. My father and brother exchanged a small, unspoken nod. Even my grandmother's hand, resting over her childhood version's hand, looked soft and protective.

"I see now," I whispered, "that coping and surviving isn't about going it alone. It's about reclaiming joy, safety, and love across time. We are not broken. We are whole as long as we are together."

Judith counted us back slowly, and as the memory dissolved, I felt a lingering sense of serenity. The heaviness in my chest had lifted. We had met the children we once were, and in doing so, we had freed ourselves. We didn't erase the past; we acknowledged it. We leaned on one another. I saw that resilience runs in our family's blood.

My mother didn't have to carry everything alone. My grandmother's silence wasn't rejection. It was memory. I wasn't the problem: I was part of the healing. I could feel proud instead of guilty. My younger brother, Masoud, saw hope.

We all recognized how courage, connection, and love could survive even the heaviest shadows. Now, when I imagine the tree, I see my family sitting with me beneath its branches. I still struggle sometimes, but I know I don't have to carry everything alone. The gardens of past and present remind me that together, we endure.

Through the following four sessions, we visited earlier times, centuries ago. In one, we lived in a palace with my father, Aziz, as the prince and head of the family. Sunlight bounced off marble floors, servants carried trays of fruit, and laughter echoed in halls that smelled of jasmine. In another, I was a captured adolescent, forced into violence under threat to my family. Suddenly, my choices in the present made sense. My former friends at school, the "misfits and bullies," were echoes of survival strategies from past lives. Being with them, even in ways I didn't like, had felt safe. Now I understood why I had sought that refuge in this lifetime.

In our debriefing sessions, it became clear that we had all been together many times and in many different circumstances. We were beginning to understand why we had all come together again in this lifetime. We realized that our important work together was just beginning.

Reader Takeaway

Ahmad's story demonstrates the power of intergenerational healing, similarly to Carl's experience (Chapter 3). Trauma often passes down in silence, but safety, resilience, and trust can be passed forward to future generations through presence and connection. When a younger generation acknowledges and comforts the older, it disrupts cycles of fear.

Healing is not erasing the past. It is transforming its perspective from trauma to strength (Landau & Stanton, 1983). The pain doesn't disappear but becomes a memory. Memory can be revisited with the acknowledgment that the trauma has contributed to the present and made us what we are today: resilient, strong, and connected. Natalie (Chapter 2) had lots of work to do with James after the hypnotherapy, but her pathway had become clear in a similar way.

Significantly, Ahmad's personal history was interwoven with family trauma, loss, unresolved grief, multiple transitions, and unspoken secrets that echoed across generations.[1] His cultural identity, his sense of purpose, and his internal resilience were all flavored by this collective history.

This family, like our families in the earlier chapters, learned that resilience is shared, not held separately by individuals. By exploring past and present, and sharing each other's voices and experiences, they found practical and emotional ways to improve their lives. PLRH revealed patterns across lifetimes that mirrored their current struggles. It helped each member understand their behaviors and alleviated their guilt (Boszormenyi-Nagy & Spark, 1973). Collectively, they could now build a safer, more hopeful future.

Note

1 YouTube video by Judith Landau, "Family Stories, Secrets, and Survival," January 25, 2013.

Chapter 6

Silent Control

Some hungers are older than this lifetime
Whispers of sacrifice and sorrow passed through generations,
silent yet unyielding, until the soul remembers and begins to heal.

Author

Ana was 17 when her parents, José and Yolanda, brought her to see us. This was one of the few times since their divorce that her parents had come together in a common mission. Her father had remarried and her mother was still a single parent. They had divorced when Ana was 12, and even though she lived with her mother, both parents were devoted and terrified in equal measure. Their daughter was approaching adulthood, and with that came the looming fear that she would soon have full legal autonomy and that she might use that autonomy against her own well-being. They sensed that they were running out of time. From the beginning of the first meeting, it became apparent that Ana was at the center of the divorce triangle and that the father blamed the mother's relationship with her for the divorce.

Ana, a soft-spoken girl with delicate features and eyes that held both sharp intelligence and deep exhaustion, carried herself like someone twice her age, with the burden of the world on her shoulders. She had a very superficial relationship with her stepmother and had never completely forgiven her father for deserting her mother, the subsequent divorce, and remarriage. She was extremely close to her mother and felt that she was the only person who could help her mother cope with her depression and loneliness.

From 12 onward, Ana's life had been shaped by a punishing cycle of restriction, bingeing, and purging. This rhythm of survival seemed to come from somewhere far deeper than the struggles of adolescence and family coalitions. She had an excellent psychiatrist and a seasoned psychotherapist, both of whom understood the severity of her condition, the complexity

DOI: 10.4324/9781003636182-7

of her inner world, and the challenge of her position caught between her parents. When Ana's parents contacted us, it was not out of desperation, but hope, the quiet kind, the kind that emerges only when every other avenue has been traveled.

With the full support of her treatment team, who agreed to be present for every session if needed, Ana began a brief but profound course of Past Life Regression Hypnotherapy. Our aim was not to replace her ongoing care but to explore whether deeper, possibly hidden origins of her struggle might reveal themselves and thereby help remove the silent barriers that kept her trapped in her self-destructive cycle.

Ana, her parents, her psychiatrist, and her psychotherapist attended the first session.

Ana's Story

When I first lay back on the couch and closed my eyes, I wasn't expecting anything. At least, that's what I told everyone. The truth was, I was terrified...terrified that nothing would happen, or worse, that *too much* would.

Judith and Charlene had me practice progressive relaxation and then, once I was feeling relaxed, find my Place of Joy. I found the relaxation easy; my mind has never had trouble slipping away; it's the coming back that's hard. The room faded quickly. It always did for me. I heard Judith's voice, steady, soft, like a hand resting on my shoulder, and then I was somewhere else entirely.

"I'm...I'm outside," I said. "It's hot. Dry. My clothes feel stiff." I heard my mother suck in a breath beside me. I recognized her sound even through my trance. "I'm older," I said. "Late twenties maybe. My hands are rough. I keep wiping sweat off my forehead." My voice trembled. "I'm hungry. So hungry that my stomach hurts."

Then came the moment I didn't want to say out loud. "I am dying," I whispered. "Not from soldiers or bombs. I died because...I stopped feeding myself."

I remember how silence fell over the therapy room, thick as smoke, as I continued, "I have three little ones. They're thin but...I'm trying. I give them everything. I pretend I'm not hungry, so they don't worry. I'm not sure I can keep them alive."

I don't eat unless they leave scraps. Sometimes I fake a full stomach, so they won't ask. They didn't ask to be brought into this life. It's my responsibility to keep them alive.

During the debriefing, I remembered hearing my therapist quietly crying. "Ana," she said softly, her voice trembling, "what you're describing... it's an act of love, but also of disappearance. Even here, in this lifetime, you try to make yourself smaller so others can have more. You don't have to do that anymore. Not here."

My mother, Yolanda, said, "I could barely breathe. Watching your child starve herself in this life is unbearable. But hearing her describe starving in another lifetime, a lifetime where she did it out of love, out of duty, something inside me broke."

Then I heard my father's quiet voice, "She's always carried too much responsibility, even as a child. She has always felt responsible for you!"

In the second session, I dropped into a hypnotic state even faster. This time, the darkness felt different. It was quieter, like a room where someone had been waiting. I felt smaller, much smaller.

"I'm a child," I said. "Six, maybe seven." My legs in the memory felt like sticks. My stomach felt like a hollow drum.

"I'm cold," I murmured. "There's no food. My mother keeps saying things will get better. I don't think I'll make it this time."

My father was supposed to bring home food. My mother is sobbing that he is with his floozy, and she's sure that he's feeding her and their illegitimate children with whatever money is left after his bingeing.

Charlene asked me to go to the next significant moment.

I'm excited, my seventh birthday is tomorrow. My mother promised me that I can invite two friends to celebrate. The door opens and I can't wait to see what my father has brought me. He bursts into the room screaming at my mother,

"Why can't you ever get things right! Where is my beer?"

He throws the empty pitcher at her, and it shatters on the wall. My mother yells back,

"There wasn't any more money for beer. You said you would get paid today and bring a treat for Ana's birthday."

He grabbed her by the shoulders and shook her,

"You are useless and I'm leaving."

He threw her onto the floor and I felt my stomach contract with fear. The scene was one I had experienced many times. It always ended the same way. My father storms out, my mother is weeping, and I'm the only person who can comfort her. I hold her close, as I do each time, and she says,

"I'm so lucky to have you! Nobody else cares whether I live or die."

I feel my whole body contracting with a sense of pride and simultaneously overwhelming responsibility.

Judith asked me to float out of my body to watch from above.

The picture unfolded slowly, painfully.

I said very softly, "I'm not in the scene. I'm floating above it." Everything seemed dark and far away.

"There's a girl. Thin. Small. She's stealing bread from a food stall when no one's looking. She's terrified. Not because it's wrong, but because she thinks she doesn't deserve it. But she convinces herself that it is the right thing to do because she must save her family."

I'm home again. I've eaten, and I feel good. I was able to give some to my mother and the baby. But my stomach is still hurting, now not from hunger but from being too full! I feel as though I'm going to explode. I rush to the latrine and rid myself of the offending burden, and my stomach is back to normal.

Once again, when I find food, I eat too much, too fast, and I must get rid of it! But at least my mother and little sister won't go hungry again. At least I'm there to take care of them both.

Judith's soft voice counting, "*one...two...three...*" a click of fingers, then, *"go to the next significant moment."*

Then I saw myself lying on a sack on a wooden floor, shivering from the bitter cold and the gnawing pain of hunger. I was alone, waiting for someone, I think my husband, to return with food.

After what seemed to be an eternity, I heard the creaking of the old door, and my husband, young but wrinkled from starvation, came over to my body. He started to weep soundlessly, without tears, and I realized that I was no longer alive.

Charlene's quiet, steady voice asked, "*Ana, what happens next?*"

My husband doesn't say anything. He just... takes the bread out of his pocket.

I watched as tears slid from the corners of my closed eyes as I watched from above. "He gives the bread to the baby he's holding instead of to me." I am aware that he is doing the very best he can.

During our second debriefing session, my therapist said,

"This is the origin of the observer role. Ana, you learned early, maybe across many lifetimes, that food, love, and nurturance belong to others. Your survival pattern was watching, not receiving. You learned not to expect anything from others, only that your role was to give and not expect to receive."

When I went to my third hypnotherapy session, as soon as I relaxed, ready for the hypnosis, I felt a heaviness settle on my chest.

"I'm older, maybe a teenager. Same lifetime as when I was the mother of the three little ones." I could feel my fingers curling slightly with commitment. "I'm promising myself something."

Charlene asked, "*What is your promise?*"

"I will never let a child go hungry. Even if I must give up everything."

When we debriefed, my father José pressed his hands to his eyes, saying,

"Dios mío... when is my child going to learn that she is worth something, worth feeding, being cared for, and worth keeping alive?!"

My psychiatrist murmured, "This is a binding vow, the belief that became fused with your identity. It explains your compulsive self-denial."

My therapist added, "A vow like this doesn't just disappear," she added. "It must be untangled. Rewritten."

During that session, something shifted. I felt it before anyone said another word.

"I don't have to do this anymore," I said. "I don't have to starve for anyone. I am not unimportant. I'm not disposable. I'm not in a war. I'm not a child alone. I'm here." Everything around me suddenly looked sharp, clear, especially my hands.

"These hands don't have to feed anyone but me. They don't have to hug everyone else unless they also hug me."

My psychiatrist leaned forward, thoughtfully. "This is a cognitive shift we rarely see without years of work. If Ana can hold onto the insight that she is no longer responsible for anyone else's survival, it will change the foundation of treatment."

My therapist added, "And it gives us a doorway, a way to help her create safety around nourishment instead of fear; a way to rewrite the vow."

At that point, my mother broke down completely. My father reached out to me and said,

"Yes, mi amor. Just you. You get to live and be loved this time." And for the first time in years, I believed I could.

I commented to everyone, "I didn't know that food could feel like permission. I didn't know it could feel like choosing to stay alive rather than proving something."

Later, my family saw that meals were still hard, but now I felt that each mouthful was a step forward rather than a battlefield.

Team Closure Meeting several months after three hypnotherapy sessions with the following debriefings:

Ana's psychotherapist said, "Trauma has layers. What Ana revealed is that some layers aren't born in this lifetime at all. What matters is that the emotional truth was real; the terror of scarcity, the belief that she had to disappear so others could live. And the belief that others would only survive if she took care of them instead of herself. Once she named those truths, we could finally help her challenge them. Her eating disorder was loyalty to an old story. What heals someone like Ana is not only nourishment, it's permission. Permission to live. Permission to take up space. Permission to belong to a world where hunger is no longer currency."

Her psychiatrist added, "Regression doesn't replace clinical work, but in Ana's case, it illuminated it. For years we had treated her symptoms. Now we understand the origin of her alarm system. She was protecting an unconscious belief that if she ate, someone else wouldn't and might die. Once that belief surfaced, the pattern unraveled. Her improvement wasn't sudden or mysterious. It was clarity. The first time that her mind and body aligned in wanting to survive."

He continued, adding, "Ana stepped out of this chapter of her life not with a sense of being cured but awakened. She carried forward not only her own strength, but the hard-earned understanding that hunger and fullness no longer had to define her and that she was no longer responsible for anyone else or their relationships. And with a clearer path before her, she finally began to choose herself."

During a later meeting, her psychiatrist noted, "Ana's sensory recall across regressions was remarkable." Temperature, texture, and the emotional imprint of each scene. It's as though her nervous system was holding entire lifetimes of scarcity and fear and releasing them piece by piece (Pohl, 2012; Porges, 2011). And it explains why conventional interventions only helped partially. Now that her root beliefs are exposed (the vows and old loyalties), we can target the true origin of her fear around nourishment and being loved. It explains the triangulation of being caught between her parents and helps us identify the next focus of our work together.

Another pivotal aspect of her healing was the family therapy. Both parents made a commitment to keep her out of the middle of their battle and to work on resolving their triangulation of her. That resulted in her being free of the responsibility to keep her mother alive. It also allowed her to develop a relationship with her stepmother and stepsiblings, and to become part of a large, healthy, talkative family with three healthier parents.

Reader Takeaway

With the insights gathered through our collaborative work, Ana's psychiatrist and psychotherapist were able to adjust the treatment plan for her eating disorder with a new sense of clarity.[1] The addition of family therapy sessions helped her separate her present identity from the echoes of her past, teaching her that caring for herself was not selfishness, but freedom and claiming the right to live and be loved.

Her parents, including her stepmother, were instructed to establish a meal plan in which one or the other of them fed her small bites until she asked for more. Their collaborative biopsychosocial (Engel, 1977) participation in loving and feeding her changed the legacy of the intergenerational coalition (Sim et al., 2009).

Ana participated in 12-Step meetings and began the slow process of self-forgiveness and building real friendships, beginning with her new family. She started to let others into her private emotional world and to understand the importance of asking for help and letting others support her. She was no longer alone.

In later sessions, Ana described sensations she had never articulated: the metallic taste of hunger, the scratch of coarse fabric, the dull ache of watching others eat. The relief of vomiting out the excess. Bringing these details to light helped free her from the ghosts that had once dictated her relationship with food. Her freedom to be loved allowed her to begin to enjoy being fed.

Over the following months, Ana's health improved. She began eating more reliably. The compulsion to purge lessened. She started speaking about her future – attending university, traveling abroad, and friendships she wanted to deepen. Each revelation became a thread woven into her recovery, threads of past lives, present courage, and a future she could now imagine. And with that deeper understanding, Ana firmly stepped into a life where sustenance was not sacrifice, but self-love.

There is no simple ending to a story like Ana's. Healing is rarely linear, and she still had work ahead of her. But what changed was profound: She no longer saw and fought her body as an enemy. She understood that the hunger she feared did not belong solely to this life, and that she now had the power to choose differently.[2] Once she understood the origin of her need to save her mother and her obligation to hate her father, she was able to establish healthy relationships with both parents and her stepmother.[3]

As we have seen in all our chapters, some burdens are carried across lifetimes. Some patterns cling to the soul until they are seen, acknowledged, and released. For Ana, bringing those hidden histories into the light allowed her to reclaim control; not through silence or starvation, but through compassion for herself and others. She saw that the cycle that had once defined her could now begin to heal.

In many ways, Ana's freedom to love and be loved came through an understanding of the past like Charlene's experience in Chapter 9 and Carl's desperation and unresolved grief in Chapter 3. For all of them, the insight gained through hypnotherapy allowed them to believe that love was possible and that they were lovable.

Notes

1 Anorexia nervosa is a complex multifactorially determined eating disorder with psychological, biological, environmental, familial, and sociocultural factors (Rikani et al., 2013; Lock, 2015). The role of family factors has been increasingly recognized both in the complex pathogenic and maintenance mechanisms and in the effectiveness of the therapeutic strategies for patients with anorexia nervosa (Lyke and Matsen, 2013; Anastasiadou et al., 2014; Lock, 2015).

2 Family therapy, which includes fathers as well as the mothers, has achieved the most relevant evidence of effectiveness (evidence type I) (Fisher et al., 2018; Couturier et al., 2013; Minuchin and Fishman, 1981) and is considered the first-line treatment for teens under the age of 19 (Le Grange et al., 2010; Lock, 2011; Hay et al., 2014). However, some recent studies showed that other therapies, such as adolescent-focused therapy (AFT) (Fitzpatrick et al., 2010), can also be just as effective. Along with the well-established Family Based Therapy (FBT) (Le Grange and Eisler, 2009; Murray and Le Grange, 2014), other family

therapeutic approaches based on different theoretical matrixes have also shown good evidence of effectiveness: This is the case of the psychodynamic therapy based on the intra-family relationships created by the French group of the Montsouris from Paris (Godart et al., 2012).

3 The parental couple's participation and involvement of the whole family in the adolescent's treatment process is recognized as a key prognostic factor (National Institute for Health, and Care Excellence [NIHCE], 2004; American Psychiatric Association, 2006; Hay et al., 2014; Espie and Eisler, 2015; Herpertz-Dahlmann et al., 2015; Lock, 2015).

Chapter 7

Your Mother Will Be the Death of Our Marriage

Some battles in love are not born of the present,
but echoes of old wounds passed down like heirlooms
until two souls brave enough to remember, choose to break the chain.

Author

Michael and Laura requested Past Life Regression Hypnotherapy to explore why, despite loving each other deeply, they kept getting into intense disagreements. Married for three years, they still loved each other; however, they felt they were destroying their relationship with stingingly harsh and cutting arguments. As they sat opposite on the couch, there was a noticeable distance between them, not only physically but emotionally.

This young couple was desperately searching for hope and guidance, either to mend their relationship or face the reality of a separation. They had not yet committed to having children and wanted to be more certain about their marriage before taking this major step. Michael was experiencing waves of depression, obsessive thoughts, and actions that left him restless and exhausted. He refused to take antidepressant medication, stating that he did not like the side effects or the way they made him feel. Instead, he felt that if his wife only complied with his demands, they could both be happy again.

Laura had learned to be silent through a childhood governed by strict rules and complete obedience to parental demands. Early in the marriage, she had no problem acquiescing to Michael's rules, but after a while, she realized that she was repeating her childhood pattern and started to challenge his demands. She no longer wanted to anticipate, comply, and if necessary, hide her own feelings to please her husband.

Why, when we love each other so deeply, do we keep wounding each other? Is there something in our past that is driving this process?

DOI: 10.4324/9781003636182-8

Arguments that were loud and biting were followed by silence, shame, and the ache of not being understood. As they spoke about their story, I had a vision of Michael's mother towering over them, a silent judgmental presence. Michael was the oldest of three boys and he explained that his mother had always adored him and called him her "golden child."

As he spoke, he realized that some of Laura's complaints about his mother might be justified since she could never see anything wrong with his behavior. It was this dynamic that had led to endless sibling battles with his brothers, and he now recognized that this pattern was being repeated in his marriage.

Michael's mother treated Laura as an intruder. Her voice was always unnecessarily sharp; her criticisms masked as compassionate support. She believed that she was responsible for training Laura to be the wife her son deserved and felt that Laura was falling far short of her expectations.

Michael acknowledged that he expected Laura to be obedient, as did his mother. He was always surprised when she questioned one of his requests or decisions. It had not occurred to him that he was treating her as a child, or a younger sibling, not as a wife.

As the first session unfolded, it became clear that with the death of her alcoholic husband when the boys were young, Michael's mother had elevated him to the position of her missing partner. She had never remarried, and both she and his brothers looked to Michael for approval. They regarded him as the "head of the family."

Michael, having been elevated to the parental position as a ten-year-old, was out of his depth and had learned to manage conflict by dictating his expectations and believing that they should be followed without question.

Michael's Story

During our first hypnotherapy session, Judith invited us to be together. Laura found her 'Place of Joy' on a trail among the towering redwoods. She described the air as fragrant and cool with channels of golden light piercing the canopy like blessings from above. She told us that each step she took along the trail felt like a release, as though the forest itself was absorbing her burdens. The redwoods stood as guardians; ancient, steady, whispering that she was safe, that she belonged. She felt her heart soften, her body lighten, and the strict rules of her childhood dissolved into the vastness of the trees. She felt that the redwoods were telling her:

You are strong. You are rooted. You can reach upward.

My 'Place of Joy' was very different, yet equally profound. I found comfort beneath a willow tree by a stream. The willow's branches bent low, offering shelter as the stream bubbled softly. I sat with my back against the tree trunk and felt its strength grounding my restless mind. I was seen, not as the golden child my mother expected, but simply as myself.

Judith's voice guided us, *"On my count of three, go to a place in the past where the two of you were together."*

Laura commented in a soft voice, "I see a grand house. We live there. I walk through the large wooden front doors. The house is vast with rooms and tall windows... but it feels cold."

My grandmother walks through the halls like a queen. She looks at me and asks me accusingly why my little sister's clothes are so dirty and unkempt. I explain that we've been playing in the garden. Her disapproval makes me feel bad about myself and I feel the tears coming. I must get away from her.

As my little sister walks away in tears, I hear myself interrupting, "You're my little sister and I think you're perfect just as you are! Go and get cleaned up right away so you're not in trouble anymore." I realize I am seeing my sibling in a life many years ago, and so even back then, my role was as her protector.

> *One...two...three...go to the next significant moment in time when the two of you are together again.*

I am looking down at my body. I see a wizened old man. My aged mother is yelling at me and threatening to strike me if I don't bring her dinner on time. She reminds me loudly that the soup must still be steaming hot. I cringe, but rush to listen to her as my dear wife stands silent and still beside me, frozen by my mother's cruel words.

> *One...two...three...click*,

I see Laura and I are together, but Laura is my daughter. My father is furious that I have produced yet another daughter, number 5, when I promised him a son! I am filled with shame even though I had no control over her gender. Once again, I have disappointed him!

In Judith's debriefing session a week later, both Laura and I were able to see how we were re-enacting scenes from our past, and that we were able to make a commitment to do things differently in the future. However, my brave plan to stand up to my mother was short-lived. There were too many years and lifetimes to change.

During the week while we waited for our next session with Judith, I began to have flashbacks, and I would wake from sleep feeling abjectly ashamed and not sure why. What had happened? What had I dreamt? Laura said that on occasion, I would be drenched in sweat and shaking with fear or dread. She told me it was very hard for her to wake me up. Needless to say, we were both looking forward to finding more answers in our next session.

Our second hypnotherapy session started with both of us returning to a lifetime where we were running a family bakery while also managing our two young children. We had to wake early in the morning to begin preparing the dough. My father was the owner of the bakery, which he had started single-handedly.

In the future, we hoped to own the business outright, but now we managed the bakery and did all the work to take the burden away from my father. However, he would not let go and was unhappy with our management and everything else we did in our lives. He would come down to the kitchen and throw things at both of us – even if one of the children was watching. This time, I stood amidst shards of broken bowls, feeling demeaned as he yelled at me,

"Why are you so incompetent? How can you ever take over the business? You and your children will starve unless you start to learn how to do things properly!"

I hated that my children and wife were seeing me in that position. My father seemed unfazed by my discomfort, which upset me even more.

As I returned from my hypnotic state to the reclining chair in the therapy room, I realized that my father in that lifetime was my mother in this one. It felt as though I would never get away from her. I was overwhelmed by a strange combination of comfort and sameness, along with dread that nothing would ever change.

Thinking about our hypnotherapy experiences and debriefing sessions, I realized that in every lifetime we revisited, regardless of our relationship with each other and my mother, my relationship with Laura was always denigrated by my mother. Prior lifetimes revealed a continuing pattern of abuse across generations. In more than one lifetime, my mother was verbally abusing me and my wife about our approach to raising our children. She was also especially acerbic about my wife's incompetence in the kitchen and the home, just as she was in this lifetime: Just as my father in a past life had been.

Following Judith's guidance, we continued to keep our journals, recording our feelings, dreams, and the subtle shifts we noticed between sessions. Yet each night, upon returning home, we found ourselves drawn once more into our familiar pattern of heated arguments. We could not stop wounding each other with sharp words despite our shared intention to be kind and never hurt each other again.

Laura's story also unfolded during our hypnotherapy sessions. She visited a lifetime where she had been picked to marry a young man of wealth, who she recognized as me. My parents had decided it was time for me to take a wife and claim my place in the family business. Laura was one of many young girls wishing for the opportunity to gain my attention and my standing in life.

My mother told Laura that she should be grateful that I chose her. While talking, she unconsciously stroked my hair with a proud expression of ownership and authority. It made me feel small, young, and invisible.

I heard my mother's voice as she instructed us about our upcoming marriage.

"You must remember that even though you are old enough to get married, that doesn't mean that you know what you know enough to manage a family. I am still the head of the household, and I expect you both to obey me." She added, "Laura, you are still you and uneducated and will need to be taught how to behave in order to become a deserving member of our family."

I felt embarrassed and triangulated between these two women. I wanted to protect Laura, but once again I was afraid. I have always been afraid. My mother's reactions have ruled my life.

Between hypnotherapy sessions, I had a dream where I was once again the husband, but I had spent most of my life in prison for embezzlement. At no time in my life had I made good. I remained the black sheep and outcast of our family. In this dream, it became apparent to me that it was not only Laura who was not good enough. Neither was I!

As we worked through our dreams and hypnotherapy experiences, Judith explained what happened when there was unresolved grief in a family, and a young child steps up to fill an adult role. She explained that there was nothing that I could have done to feel competent in a role well beyond my years and level of maturity. The fact that my mother had never remarried left me in that role long-term, which is why Laura was regarded as an intruder and a threat.

Once we both understood our roles in the family's intergenerational pattern of loss and unresolved grief, we were able to change not only our expectations of one another, but also my mother's understanding of our love for one another. She became more at ease with Laura, and she began to socialize and ultimately to date again. The process was gradual but consistent, and Laura and I realized that our having children and raising them differently had the power to change the intergenerational pattern of loss and abuse.

As my mother's behavior softened, my brothers realized that their addictive behavior was part of the intergenerational pattern and that they no longer had to stay home and be dysfunctional. After a couple of years of their own therapy and 12-Step meetings, they were able to move into recovery and develop their own long-term relationships.

Reader Takeaway

Michael and Laura's experience provides an example of how identifying past relationship patterns and traumas can directly impact our lives in the present time (Boszormenyi-Nagy & Spark, 1973). This awareness can provide resolution and the stimulus to change our behavior. When family members discover these insights together, the family can move forward with understanding and positive intention.

Despite their history, or because of it, these two people kept finding each other again and again. They now had an opportunity to overcome the overwhelming burden of the past. During the hypnotherapy process, it became apparent that, given the opportunity, they were trying to mend their historic rift. They now realized that they could choose to draw on the strength of their intergenerational patterns rather than repeating the vulnerability (Landau, 2018). They began to understand that they could choose to change the future intergenerational patterns.

In some ways, their story is like that of Ana (Chapter 6) and her parents. She was caught in a similar triangle between her parents, and only when she gained insight did she realize that she did not have to participate in the triangular coalition. She could then begin to heal.

Michael and Laura needed to recognize the power of the intergenerational coalition of mother and son and how Laura was caught in the triangle (Minuchin & Fishman, 1981). Once they gained this insight, they were free to form a lasting bond. Another similarity was that neither had to alienate the person with whom they were bound in coalition: They could all develop loving, lasting relationships.

This family's remembered scenes were not random. They were echoes of the past. The soul remembers as the nervous system remembers. The mind, body, and soul become a map of what has been and what could be repeated in the future. These lifetimes are never random. They are mirrors. Each reflects the same wound: love entangled with control, intimacy poisoned by shame.

The mother's grip was not just one woman's cruelty; it was an archetype, a pattern carried across generations. The son had learned that love meant domination in the same way that Ana (Chapter 6) learned that love meant caretaking and sacrifice. Laura had learned that love meant submission. Together, each group reenacted the dance of power and silence, storm and retreat.

This is the shadow side of enmeshment. When a parent does not release their child into adulthood, whether because of the need for control or, in this case, to fill an overwhelming loss beyond their control, a template for dysfunction is laid down (Seaburn, et al., 1995). The child learns that love is control. That loyalty means obedience and sacrifice. That disobedience means a lack of love and the right to be nurtured. That rage is a form of intimacy. It is only by resolving the unresolved grief and the re-assigning of roles, that healing can occur. If this does not happen, the pattern continues across generations.

This couple's story is not unique. Many of us carry the weight of generations. Emotional, physical, and financial abuse can echo through time, disguised as personality traits or "just how things are." But they are not fixed. They are patterns. And patterns can be changed. This couple's journey is a testament to the strength of how love and awareness can impact intergenerational patterns and make it possible to choose to change them.

Chapter 8

See No Evil, Hear No Evil, Speak No Evil

Silence is not the absence of truth
Only the place where truth hides when it feels unsafe.
Families repeat what they cannot speak.
Only when seen and heard can the cycle break.

Author

A South African Hindu man, Ravi, sought help for his wife, Meera (known as Amaa or mother), and their daughter, Anika, aged 15, both of whom had been experiencing episodes of dissociative blindness, dizziness, and deafness for over two years. Despite numerous visits to physicians and emergency rooms, no medical solution had been found. Doctors and psychotherapists had diagnosed the symptoms as psychosomatic, conversion reactions from stress, but their efforts to identify their origin had failed. The family was convinced that something terrible was wrong with both mother and daughter and sought consultation to find the truth and the solution. There was a second child, the youngest sibling, Arjun, age 12. He was 'the Prince' and "could do no wrong."

Tension in the household had escalated when Ravi's mother Prya arrived from India. (Prya was called Mata by the family, which means grandmother). She had not given her blessings to her son's marriage to Meera and had never accepted her as her daughter-in-law. Mata (Prya) began to live with them quietly, but her presence was oppressive. Subtle, manipulative, and cruel when Ravi wasn't looking, she silently targeted Meera and Anika, criticizing, belittling, and undermining them. Meanwhile, she spoiled Arjun, indulging his every wish and making him feel invincible. Ravi, who had been in the same elevated role as Arjun in his family of origin, saw only her outwardly warm behavior toward Arjun and blamed Meera whenever tensions surfaced. He believed that Meera was overreacting and causing trouble. Meera's mother, Soramini (Dadee – another name

DOI: 10.4324/9781003636182-9

for grandmother), lived nearby and offered emotional support, but she could not intervene in the complex household dynamics.

The family sought hypnotherapy as a last resort, an attempt to uncover the hidden roots of their suffering and find a path toward healing.

Ravi's Story

I thought I was holding the family together. I worked long hours, tried to provide, tried to keep the peace. I didn't see how much my mother's (Mata's) presence hurt Meera and the kids. I saw her spoiling Arjun, thought it was normal, and blamed Meera for all the tension. I felt trapped between my mother and my wife and between tradition and love.

I was unable to protect anyone fully. My mother-in-law, Soramini (Dadee), was 'a constant thorn in my side' because she always took the side of Meera and Anika and blamed me for not being supportive of them. She also insisted that I was spoiling my son, Arjun.

Meera (Amaa – Mother)

Every time I tried to talk about what was happening, I felt like my voice disappeared. I would complain about her (my mother-in-law, Mata), and my husband Ravi would say,

> "She's only being kind to Arjun. You're overreacting."

But it wasn't kindness to both children. It was kindness to Arjun, but simultaneously cruelty to my daughter Anika and me. Mata always wrapped her mean comments in charm and Ravi couldn't see through it. Arjun… he was always safe. Always untouchable. And Anika and I both suffered in silence.

Anika

I felt trapped in a cage I couldn't see. I knew my Mata hated me, but I couldn't say it out loud. If I spoke, my Papa would blame my mom, my Amaa, and I'd be the problem. So, I closed my eyes, sometimes for hours. Other times, I couldn't hear her. It was the only way I could survive. Arjun never had to hide. He could do no wrong. I hated him for it, but I loved him too. He was my little brother. I didn't understand how he could be safe while Amaa and I weren't.

Arjun

At first, I didn't notice the cruelty. My grandmother, Mata, smiled at me, let me have candy whenever I wanted, and laughed at my jokes. But sometimes

I saw Amaa crying, or Anika staring at the floor. I didn't understand why they were sad. I felt guilty, but I didn't know what I could do. I just wanted everyone to be happy.

Soramini (Dadee – Grandmother)

The way that my son-in-law Ravi treated Arjun seemed very unfair to me. He always gave him the best parts of the chicken at dinner and forgave him for his rude behavior toward me and his mother.

I realized that Ravi had been treated as the prince of his family, and that he was continuing the tradition in his new family. I tried repeatedly to talk to him about his favoritism, but my words fell on deaf ears.

Ravi

Judith began our first hypnotherapy session by guiding each of us to find our 'Place of Joy,' a place of beauty and peace where we felt safe and grounded. She told us that we could find a place that we all shared, or we could each have our own sacred place.

I remember my wife Meera describing herself in her childhood home in Durban, sunlight pooling on terracotta tiles, jasmine trailing in the air. The hot, humid tropical day making her feel languid and relaxed.

My daughter Anika imagined herself in a quiet garden behind her school, a soft breeze in her hair, sunlight on her face. My son Arjun pictured himself playing cricket under a mango tree, the smell of earth and grass grounding him. He said he was waiting for the rain to come out so that the monkeys would come to play with the green mangoes.

I remembered how I felt in my father's workshop, with his tools neatly arranged, where he always made me feel capable of doing anything I wanted to do.

My wife's mother, Soramini, chose a quiet beach behind the home where she had grown up, saying that the light off the ocean had always made her feel that she was at peace with the world.

After we had all selected our individual 'Places of Joy,' we were ready to move forward with our hypnotherapy journey. Judith's voice was calm and deliberate,

> *Close your eyes. Take a deep breath. Imagine stepping back in time to the moment your body or anyone else in the family first began to respond with blindness or deafness. Watch, observe, float above your body if the situation feels too intense.*

Meera spoke first. "I'm in a dark hallway. I can't see… everything is gray. I hear someone talking. I think it is my mother-in-law, but the voice is quite different. It is an old woman's voice, husky from smoking too much. I think she is saying that I should be whipped, but I don't understand the words. I feel dizzy, like I'm floating away." Judith encouraged her to float upward.

> *Watch from above. You're safe. Notice what's happening without needing to react.*

Meera continued, "The old woman is laughing at me and my discomfort. She seems to have won an argument and everyone in the room is blaming me for somebody's death. I have no idea who died. I think we are in a courtroom but not like one from today. From the décor, I think it must be in the 1600's, but I can't see a date anywhere. I'm terrified and when the judge asks me to speak, I have no voice."

Judith's voice brought me back into my body, and as she asked me to go to the next significant moment, *"one...two...three...click,"* Meera continued, tears streaming, "I see myself as a young woman again. I'm in a crowded, dark place. People are yelling, fighting, and pushing each other to get to the front of the crowd. I am back on a platform with my hands and feet tied. I have no idea where they are trying to go or what is happening. Are they trying to watch what is going to happen to me? I can't make a sound. Mata is there... She is the judge leading the ceremony."

Meera continued, "I must have done something terrible... I feel invisible. I have to disappear to survive whatever they are going to do to me."

Mata interrupted. "You committed a murder. You started a fire in your home that burned your husband to death. You must die."

Judith asked me to, *"Float out of your body and watch the scene from above."*

As I watched the scene, I saw myself frozen in time and voiceless. I wanted to shout, "I was just defending myself. My husband was beating me to death. I had no choice. You must listen to me. This is not my fault. I'm innocent." But no sound came out. I was sentenced to death.

During the debriefing the week following the family hypnotherapy session, Mata explained that she had also seen herself in Merra's hypnosis session. She said that Meera's husband had been me, Ravi. She was the judge who sentenced my beloved Meera to death.

Mata, my mother, realized that her dependence on me and refusing to see anything that I did wrong was her attempt to assuage the guilt of not having been able to save me from being burned to death in that previous lifetime.

In our third meeting, the second family hypnotherapy session, the focus was on the children. When it came to Arjun's turn, he hesitated, then explained, "I just want to leave the room when there is unpleasantness. I hate that my Amaa and my Mata are always at each other. I love them both and they both treat me really well. I don't like it, but I don't know how to help them."

During hypnosis, when Judith asked me to go from my 'Place of Joy' to the next significant moment, I saw two young girls in a classroom. I said,

> I think they are sisters. they both look so scared. The teacher is standing over them with a ruler with steel edging. I think he is planning to cane them. I don't know what they've done. I want to help, but I don't know how. I think they are my Amaa and Mata…they have been arguing, and the teacher is angry with them. Now that he wants to cane them, they are both standing up for each other and trying to stop him hurting the other one. They love each other!

As the session continued, I was in my father's workshop, my 'Place of Joy,' when I heard Judith say,

> *Go to the next significant moment where you are all together and Meera or Anika starts to lose their capacity to speak, hear, or move.*

I saw that we were all together again. I was with my wife and my daughter, walking along a dusty road, barefoot, carrying what little we had. Our littlest son (I think he's Arjun) was running behind us.

I am a young man of about 35. "My wife and my little daughter are clinging to my hands. I think they are Meera and Anika. We are so afraid! There is a man chasing us. I think he is Mata. I think he wants to kill us all. I don't know what we've done. We have nothing he could want from us. My little daughter is crying, and I… I can't stop it. I can't keep her safe."

Anika echoed, "It's like I've been there before. I'm scared… but I know we survive somehow. I can't see anything; I can't speak. But, somehow, I know that my mother and father will save me."

She continues, "I think Amaa is my mother and Papa is the father. Is the strange man, Mata?"

Arjun, "I'm running behind Amaa, Papa, and Anika. I'm about 5 years old. I fall… but a man I don't know lifts me up. I think he is Mata. He's lifting me up, so I don't get left behind and he's offering to help the rest of the family escape. We're all together. I'm scared, but… we all survive."

Meera, "I'm terrified. I can't save my children. I can't call for help. I can't move. We're all going to die."

Mata (Prya), "I wish there were something I could do for my son and my grandchildren. I thought my coming from India would help but it hasn't."

Judith's voice asked me to float out of my body and watch the scene from a safe space.

From my safe place above the scene, I realize that the man I thought was chasing us (Mata) has picked up my littlest son, whom I recognize as Arjun. He is trying to protect us, not wanting to kill us. He is an ally, not a foe.

Mata, "You all think I'm to kill you. I'm trying to save your lives. I love you all. I just don't always know how best to show it."

Anika says, "I'm hiding behind a door. I see two women arguing. I think that they are Amaa and Mata. I can't hear their words; it's like the world has gone silent. I am 5 years old. I'm dressed in a beautiful blue dress with ribbons in my hair and shiny white shoes. I think my mother is Mata and the woman with her is my mother, Amaa. My mother has helped me dress. The other one, Amaa, is carrying a green dress and wants me to change into it."

"I think we were going to a party and maybe the party is for me. But now, I just want to run away and not hear the fighting. I have been waiting for a long time for this party, but I'm afraid that they might really hurt each other. I'm very sad because I love parties. But wait a minute, the two women have stopped fighting and are coming towards me holding hands. What is wrong? I'm really surprised because they hug me and say, Let's go to your party. You will love the presents we've brought you and we have decided when it is time for the cake, you will change into your beautiful new green dress."

After the intensity of our experience, Judith ended the session with all of us returning to our 'Places of Joy.' Relief mingled with recognition of the trauma we all carried. Judith reminded all of us to keep a journal of our memories of the hypnotherapy session and all the thoughts, dreams, and memories that had emerged since.

The following week at our debriefing session, my wife Meera spoke first, "I never realized it before, but this... this blindness and deafness, it's been happening for many lifetimes. I understand now that I've been trying to disappear in an effort to survive."

Then we heard from my daughter, Anika, "I thought it was just me... but now I see we've done this before. We all carry the past in our minds and our bodies."

My son Arjun added, "I feel guilty for being safe while you all suffered. But I also see now that I can help. I don't have to worry about protecting you from everything. I can be part of the family, and that is what I want to be."

As I listened to all of them, I realized that even when I thought I must be strong and protect my entire family, I could let go and rely on others. I didn't have to spend this lifetime making up for my past bad deeds.

I began hoping that this experience would also let Meera know that my mother is not the enemy, but that she is trying in her own way to help us all. Her tools are traditional and don't always fit the requirements of modern living. But her intentions were good.

My fear that I was the only one who could protect my family was not true. My mother, my mother-in-law, and my wife were all there with me. We have been together before, and we will be together... always. While they all shared, I began to have a better understanding of my mother's and my roles.

I shared with the family, "I see my mother's role. She's repeating her own pain, her judgment. I realize I've been silent, trying to keep the peace. I don't have to do this alone anymore. We are all together and the family understands that my mother's motives are pure. We need to help her adjust to a new culture and living situation that is still very foreign to her."

Judith reflected on what we had all experienced and shared her thoughts. *"What you experienced in regression is a map—your family patterns across generations. Your bodies expressed trauma in ways the mind could not: blindness, deafness, paralysis, dizziness, and withdrawal. Recognizing this is the first step toward breaking these cycles."*

We all spent the remainder of the debriefing session reviewing the details of our journaling and discussing ways to communicate openly. A radical act for a family used to silent endurance.

During our third hypnotherapy session, I began to understand my mother's behavior more clearly. During our family regression, my wife Meera said, "I'm a young woman again. Mata is my sister. She is older and she tends to judge me. I *have* to be perfect. Anika is hiding beside me. I can't show Mata any weakness. And Arjun... he is smiling, laughing. He's safe. I feel so small. I can't protect Anika."

Anika

"I'm very young. I've just finished a drawing. I want my aunt (who I think is Mata) to be proud of me. She ignores me. She won't even look at my picture. I can't hear her words, but I feel her judging me. Why doesn't she love me? Why can't I do anything to please her? I close my eyes... and my world goes silent. It doesn't matter. My mother is reassuring me that my aunt does love me but has very high standards. She says that her sister judges her, too."

Arjun

I am 12 years old and my team just won our soccer game. My mother is so proud of me. I think my mother is Mata. I feel very good. She says she will get me whatever I want as a prize. I look over at my little sister (who I think is Anika) and she is crying. I don't know that by my mother spoiling me, she is hurting Anika. I feel bad now, but I like her spoiling me. I don't want her to stop loving me. But I want everyone else to be safe and loved, too.

As my family shared their experiences, I realized why I've been working so hard to persuade them to get along better. I thought my silence was keeping the peace. I didn't understand that my silence meant that I was ignoring their pain. Now I understood that my silence made them unable to talk about their feelings and only increased their suffering.

When I would sit at my desk, trying to work and hear my mother's voice in the kitchen, I knew she was criticizing my wife and daughter. I felt that I couldn't stop her. My chest would get tight and I felt powerless. Now I recognized that if I spoke up, it would have been a way of protecting my wife and daughter. After the Past Life Regression Hypnosis, I realized that my mother would understand the family dynamics and accept both my criticism and my support.

During our third debriefing session, everyone in the family, including my mother, acknowledged her favoritism. She made a commitment to try to be more even-handed with the children and to stop judging my wife and my mother-in-law. She explained that she had been raised to understand that her only value in her family of origin was as a caretaker of the men, especially the boys who would ultimately be the heads of the family. She committed to expressing care and support explicitly, reducing the silent suffering of the other women.

Meera said that after the hypnotherapy, "It is hard to believe that things will change but it hurts less to talk about it aloud now that we have all shared our feelings. The fear isn't as heavy when it's shared."

Arjun contributed his feelings, "I understand that I can protect my sister and not worry any more that when I do, Mata will no longer like me. I think that there is room for both of us."

In our fourth and final hypnotherapy session, we all returned to our 'Places of Joy,' and revisited our past lives together. We witnessed several lifetimes of survival, hunger, abuse, and violence, but we were always together. I realized that our bond carried across time and lives. Whatever we did in this lifetime, while influenced by our past lives, gave us the choice to decide how we wanted to interact in this lifetime. We didn't have to repeat all the patterns of pain, but could choose the patterns of joy, connection, and love.

During our debriefing, Arjun said to me, "Papa, I understand now. Mata… she hurt Mom and Anika, but we can all be different. We can love each other and protect each other." Anika added, "We don't have to hide. I can open my eyes. I can hear. I can speak. We are together, and that is stronger than being afraid."

My wife Meera said, "I feel lighter. I don't have to disappear. I can see my children, hear them, protect them and ask Ravi for help. I can even ask Mata to be kinder to all of us. And I now understand why she has favored Ravi and Arjun. We need to love her too."

I realized that we were breaking the pattern of many generations. I saw the favoritism, the silent cruelty, and made a commitment that I would never again ignore it. We are a family, one team. We are together, and we will learn to live together without hurting one another ever again.

Judith guided us through a visualization: A sunlit garden where we could sit together, past and present selves aligned. Arjun played nearby, laughing with Anika. Meera felt empowered to set boundaries with her mother-in-law, Mata. I felt capable of protecting my family without blame or silence, and Dadee felt that she no longer had to protect her daughter and granddaughter.

The session ended with a sense of unity, recognition of broken cycles, and hope for the future.

Reader Takeaway

This chapter demonstrates how intergenerational trauma, silent suffering, and favoritism create complex family dynamics. Symptoms like dissociative blindness or deafness may appear inexplicable, but they are often expressions of traumatic relationships repeated across generations (Center for Mindful Therapy, 2025; Marschall, 2024).

Healing occurs through collective acknowledgment: seeing and being seen, hearing and being heard. Silence and unspoken pain are major mechanisms through which trauma is transmitted across generations (Clare, 2025). Even younger members, like Arjun, can gain empathy and insight, disrupting harmful cycles. Children often absorb and reenact trauma responses from previous generations, developing protective behaviors and emotional withdrawal.

Ravi learned a valuable lesson. There had been one occasion where he raised his hand to Meera as though to strike her, but he had managed to control his temper and just walk away. He understood for the first time that Meera had become frightened of him and had been unable to express any of her feelings. He committed to being available and open to her feelings, even if they were uncomfortable and involved her relationship with his mother.

The children, sensing the conflict, had developed protective mechanisms: Anika used to retreat into periods of dissociative blindness, Arjun into selective hearing and withdrawal, and Meera into silent endurance. These embodied trauma responses are consistent with how intergenerational trauma manifests somatically (Rosenthal, 2021).

Past-life regression hypnotherapy provides a bridge across time: families can witness recurring patterns, release emotional weight, and create conscious, healthier dynamics. Healing is not linear; it requires facing discomfort, acknowledging hidden dynamics, and choosing to love rather than living in fear. Family therapy and trauma-informed approaches are essential in breaking these cycles (Center for Mindful Therapy, 2025).

Ravi, Meera, Anika, Arjun, Pyra, and Soramini's journey shows that resilience is forged through awareness, connection, and shared courage. Even deeply entrenched patterns of suffering can transform into a foundation for unity, compassion, and safety (Franco, 2023).

Chapter 9

The Healing Space Between Death and Life

Some loves do not belong to this life alone.
They echo through time, shaping who we are until we remember, release, and return to ourselves.
Whole, at last.

Author

Charlene's Story

My journey into Past Life Regression Hypnotherapy (PLRH) began nearly 25 years ago, inspired by a birthday gift that would silently transform my life. The gift was Brian Weiss's book *Many Lives, Many Masters*. As I read his introduction and then each chapter, I felt something awaken within me. The stories resonated deeply, giving me a sense of recognition I could not quite explain. I began noticing subtle yet persistent patterns in my own family, recurring behaviors, emotional wounds, and personality traits that seemed to echo across generations.

What intrigued me most was the uncanny feeling of seeing myself reflected in ancestors I had never met. It was as if their unresolved stories were still alive in me. I felt as though love had been lost and longed for, repeatedly, throughout the branches of my family tree. That realization pierced and haunted me. With clarity, I saw that I was not just a witness to these patterns, but I was also someone who was following the same path. I wondered if I could shift these patterns in my own life to restore what had been fractured.

The desire to understand my life journey, as it correlated with this ancestral lineage, was emotional and frightening. I wondered if I could live up to these strong and complex people from whom I was descended. PLRH offered a path not only to insight, but to healing. With every fiber of my being, I knew I had to walk it if I hoped for a love that was both unconditional and enduring.

DOI: 10.4324/9781003636182-10

I began searching for a Past Life Regression Hypnotherapist who could help me. With a heart full of hope, I reached out to Dr. Brian Weiss's office, leaving a message to share how profoundly his book had touched me. To my astonishment, he called me back personally. His voice was warm and soothing. He was happy that his work had resonated with me so deeply and wished that it would continue to inspire my journey. At that moment, I felt something sacred unfolding. It was as if the universe had whispered, "You're on the right path."

Later, when I spoke with his assistant, she told me that Dr. Weiss never returned calls himself. Her words struck me. This wasn't just a coincidence. I felt heartbreak when she told me he was fully booked for the next year. However, just as quickly, disappointment gave way to a spark of hope. She offered to refer me to someone he trusted and who worked nearby where I lived. That someone turned out to be Dr. Judith Landau, who would later become a pivotal figure in my healing and subsequently a lifelong friend, and now my co-author.

From the moment I met Judith, I felt an inexplicable sense of familiarity. Her voice, soft, resonant, and grounded, instantly calmed my nerves. It was as though I had known her long before this lifetime. Just stepping into her space brought a wave of peace over me. Her energy was strong and nurturing, and I felt safe. By the time I sank into her deep, welcoming recliner, I could feel my defenses melting away. I was ready to start my journey.

Judith and I pieced together my family going back as many generations as I could recall. We used a genogram (a visual map of the intergenerational family or an ascending family tree). The genogram allowed us to identify intergenerational behavioral patterns and repeated physical and mental traumas. As Judith and I delved deeper, I began to see how these unconscious patterns had already started to shape my choices in life. I now had my map. The only familiar path I had was witnessing how my mother and grandmother interacted with me and each other. It was the only way I knew how to survive.

"Be quiet unless you are spoken to." "Be seen and not heard." In order to resist this way of thinking, I moved away, tried to create distance, and tried to quiet my fear. However, I always found myself back at home base, emotionally beaten and continually silenced.

My mother, a devoted registered nurse, spent her entire life caring for others. Her compassion was a gift to many, a blessing that touched neighbors, colleagues, and even the mail carrier. But for me, as a child, it was often bittersweet. I wasn't a healthy child, and her night shifts meant I was frequently left with my grandmother, with whom we lived. I felt alone, sick, frightened, and yearning for comfort. After she would leave for work, the house would fall silent, and in that silence, I felt the ache of loneliness and fear settle deep into my bones.

My mother as well as my grandmother carried an unwavering loyalty to family, no matter how they behaved. My mother was particularly loyal to my grandmother, with whom we lived. My father would visit from time to time; however, my grandmother, the matriarch, was not always welcoming to him. I admired my mother's strength about this, but felt her loneliness.

My fear was becoming my mother. I promised myself I would be different. I hoped for a love that was both unconditional and enduring. I would have my own home and be the center of my own family, placing their needs above all else. I would not feel the silent loneliness she endured. Without realizing it, I inherited her silent creed: never blame, never hurt, only sacrifice.

My own desires, my own voice, were often the price I paid to keep the peace and survive the pain of yearning for affection. It meant surviving the scars from those who took advantage of my vulnerability. And yet, in my quiet retreat from others, I began to feel everyone slipping away. The very connection I longed for seemed to dissolve. I kept returning to the same place; alone, wounded, believing that love was something reserved for others. Not for me. I had internalized the belief that I was unworthy.

In the days between my first meeting with Judith and our upcoming hypnotherapy session, my mind was a whirlwind. I felt both exhilarated and unsettled. Concentrating at work became nearly impossible. One moment, I was tempted to call Judith and beg for an earlier appointment; the next, I considered canceling altogether, afraid that hypnosis wouldn't work on me or that it *would*. The anticipation was overwhelming, and the vulnerability it stirred was a deep darkness that I could not see beyond.

I was also torn about where to focus my attention. My heart longed to understand my emotional struggle in connecting with my family, but another part of me was consumed by a man I had just met, Thomas. Our paths kept crossing, and I couldn't shake the feeling that we had known each other before. Was he somehow connected to me in a previous life? Had we once been relatives? The intensity of his presence made me question everything. Why did I feel compelled to choose between exploring my roots and unraveling the mystery of a relative stranger?

Thomas owned a cozy café in a charming nearby village. I met him there once, then again, and again. Each encounter left a lasting imprint. I could still feel the moment he first walked toward me, his energy, his gaze, the quiet familiarity. I found myself replaying that meeting, wondering what it meant. Eventually, I decided to focus on my connection with him before diving into my family's story.

When I arrived for my second session, Judith greeted me with her signature calm presence. My pulse slowed as I settled into her space, ready to uncover how Thomas fit into my life. Yet even then, I was confused. I was newly married and loved my husband deeply. So why did I feel such a profound sense of loss over someone I barely knew? Had I lost Thomas before? Why did that matter so much? The feelings made no logical sense, and I began to question myself. Was something wrong with me? The longing remained. I wanted Thomas in my life.

Judith invited me to describe my first meetings with him. Over a ten-year period, my chronic pain and medical challenges often led me to the village for physical therapy. I found myself retreating to Thomas's cozy café at the end of each session, hoping to see him. The place became a sanctuary. I was a "frequent flyer," and the staff greeted me like family. Their warmth was a relief during some of my most difficult days.

Thomas and I grew close. My friendship with him deepened as I continued my work with Judith. Thomas always made time for me, and our conversations often coincided with pivotal moments: his marriage, the birth of his children, my marital struggles, and eventually, my divorce. Only later did I realize that these encounters were not random. They aligned with the times when my pain, physically and emotionally, was at its peak.

Thomas and I spoke often about the joys and heartbreaks of my post-divorce relationship. Through it all, my bond with him remained steady. And with Thomas, there was always something more, an unspoken depth that defied explanation. There was a sense of knowing him, of remembering him, that I couldn't shake. As our friendship evolved, Thomas began to share his life story. He was happily married with two young children, and as we grew closer, he embarked on his own spiritual journey. It felt like we were walking parallel paths, each of us seeking something deeper, something timeless. It felt as though we both were pulled between the past and present.

At our next meeting, Judith began our debriefing by comparing her notes with my own reflections, dreams, and thoughts since our previous session. She described her first impression:

> *As Charlene entered my office, she was visibly anxious and eager to begin. Her speech was rapid, her energy intense, so different from our previous meeting. She launched into her story about Thomas before I could even begin the session. I gently asked her to slow down and guided her through deep, intentional breathing so we could prepare for the Past Life Regression Hypnotherapy.*[4]

Once I was calm, Judith introduced me to the hypnotherapy process. She explained that I would remain in a light hypnotic state, aware of my surroundings, sounds, and sensations. She assured me that I could return to full consciousness at any time and that she would be with me throughout the journey, ready to guide me back if needed.

She also encouraged me to journal after each session and reminded me that every hypnotherapy experience would be followed by a debriefing session, where we would compare notes and insights. Her presence, her clarity, and her care made all the difference. I felt held, supported, and ready to begin.

Judith asked me to settle into a comfortable position. For me, that meant lying back in her reclining chair, cocooned in a soft quilt wrapped around me. She began guiding me through progressive relaxation, inviting me to focus on each part of my body, feel the tension, acknowledge it, and then let it melt away.

Her voice was steady and soothing as she asked me to imagine a place of comfort, safety, beauty, and deep well-being, a place I would call my 'Place of Joy.' A sanctuary I could return to anytime I needed it. Then she asked me to describe what I saw.

A door appeared before me, vivid and unmistakable. Its shape, texture, and weight came into sharp focus as though I had touched it a thousand times before. Judith's voice dropped into a low, resonant rhythm as she slowly counted from one to ten. With each number, I sank deeper into stillness. She told me that when she reached ten, I would be able to open the door and step through.

Judith later wrote, "*It took time to help Charlene relax enough to explore her 'Place of Joy.' Her anxiety about whether hypnosis would work kept pulling her out of a relaxed state. I invited her to practice progressive relaxation with me to quiet the obsessive thoughts. This kind of initial anxiety is common, so I always allow extra time for preparation before the first hypnotherapy session. She fought against the process at first. Her breathing and pulse became very rapid, and she was clearly becoming more anxious. However, once I began the count for the hypnotherapy, she relaxed completely and was able to find her 'Place of Joy.'*"

As I opened the door, the warmth of the sun kissed my face. I felt the grainy texture of sand beneath my feet and curled my toes into its softness. Above me, the sky stretched wide and blue, dotted with scattered clouds like cotton.

Judith's voice echoed faintly in the background, counting, clicking her fingers, gently prompting me to see, hear, taste, and feel more.

Before me, the sand led into the ocean. No crashing waves, just gentle swells that shimmered under the sunlight. I sat at the water's edge, letting it lap over my toes. It was warm and soothing. I didn't want to move, but Judith kept counting, clicked her fingers, and asked me to move to the next significant moment,

What do you see, hear, taste, feel?

All around the beautiful, quiet beach, palm trees swayed. The soft breeze cooled me from the sunlight's heat. While enjoying the warmth and feeling of safety, I took a deep breath and followed the feeling of discovery into my past life.

Judith's notes continued: *"This became Charlene's 'Place of Joy' for many journeys. There was an innocence about her as she went there. Her voice lightened, her pulse slowed, and she appeared peaceful and at ease. I hated to move her away from the shore but knew that it was her respite place, and she could return at will whenever she experienced anxiety."*

Judith continued counting to three and clicking her fingers, she asked me to move to the next significant moment. My right eye began to twitch. My heart pounded in my chest. But slowly, I relaxed again into the rhythm of her voice. She asked me to look down at my feet.

"I see mid-calf black leather laced boots below a black skirt, a white ruffled blouse, and a gold stitched waist jacket. I have long, bright blonde straight hair all pulled up with loose curls, and it is pinned under a matching black hat."

I looked down at my hands, "I am wearing thin leather gloves."

At the next count of three, I found myself standing on a street corner beside a light pole. "The buildings around me look old. It is the early 1920s. My arm is linked with a man in a tan suit. He is carrying a walking cane. I feel incredibly happy. We are laughing together!"

I continued, "There are people walking up and down both sides of the street. I see a woman across the street and start moving towards her. I am not paying attention to the traffic. I feel something coming at me and then I feel a push on my back. I fall to the ground and hit the curb. My left arm is hurting. I hear many voices as people gather around me. I smell some type of motor fuel, but it is mixed with steam. It burns my nose. The pain in my arm is sharp, but I continue to try to get up. Where is the man?"

I got to my feet and saw him on the ground under the car's right front tire.

The air was filled with steam. I pushed my way through the crowd to see him, and it was Thomas! He is gasping for breath. His eyes are half closed as a tear falls down his face.

I tell him, "I love you! I am sorry! This is all my fault!"

As he took his last breath, he looked at me. Our eyes met, and then he died.

"My heart is breaking! I panic! Where do I go? What can I do?"

I hear Judith's voice guiding me: *"Float out of your body and watch the scene from above. You do not have to stay with the pain."*

Her words wrapped around me like a lifeline. I hovered above the scene, looking down at Thomas with profound sadness so deep it felt ancient. The sharp physical pain lessened.

Judith's voice anchored me, slowly drawing me back to the present. Though my eye had stopped twitching, my left arm still ached, as if echoing the trauma I had just relived. The sorrow, however, remained thick and heavy in my chest.

As I opened my eyes, Judith was there, calm and steady. The room felt both familiar and foreign, as if I had returned from a place far beyond its walls. We spoke quietly about the importance of journaling, capturing every sensation, image, and emotion that might surface before our next session.

She watched me closely, concerned about my long drive home. She offered me a glass of water and invited me to stay a while longer, helping me ground myself as I moved from the past back into the present.

My drive home felt like moving through a dream. The snow fell in thick, silent sheets, blanketing the world in white. I should have been afraid, but I wasn't. I felt strangely protected, as if something unseen was guiding me. Still, I was heavy with emotion. I wanted to cry, but the tears wouldn't come. I wanted to see Thomas, to feel his presence, but I knew I couldn't. A deep ache settled into me: I realized that I had lost him before, perhaps many times. The past clung to me like fog, making it hard to stay in the present. My senses were heightened: My body was still humming with the echoes of the session.

That night, I had a dream of being back in that time. I was in a room with high ceilings. I was sitting on the bay window ledge. I felt alone. The reality of experiencing life without Thomas was overwhelming. I stared out of the window and was engulfed in guilt and shame. This loneliness was unbearable.

The silence that consumed me only deepened the ache of his absence. He had died saving my life. As I woke from the dream, the pain was still there, not just in my arm, but in the deepest part of me. It was a pain I had carried since childhood, the same ache I could never name. Now, it had a face. A name. A story.

At our third meeting, Judith and I sat together, reviewing my journal and her notes. She explained that what happens between sessions was often just as important, if not more so, than what unfolds during the PLRH. The subconscious continues to process, to reveal, to heal. My drive home, the dream, and the lingering emotions were all part of the journey.

As we pieced everything together, the truth became clear. I finally understood why I had been so drawn to explore my connection with Thomas before turning to my family. The grief I carried wasn't just about intergenerational patterns; it was about love. A love I had lost, again and again. A love that had shaped my soul's longings. It encompassed the fear of never feeling that type of genuine happiness and unconditional love from anyone again.

Together, Judith and I began to stitch the fragments into a coherent whole. The story was no longer scattered across lifetimes. It was mine now... held, honored, and finally beginning to heal.

During our continued work together, I came to a profound realization: Across the many lifetimes I had glimpsed, it wasn't my biological family in this lifetime that held the deepest thread of continuity, it was Thomas. The lives we had shared, the children we had raised, the families we had built together across time felt like the true constant. I now understood that this lifetime was my opportunity to heal and release.

While exploring my past times with Thomas, I remembered how, as a child in this lifetime, I would climb out of my bedroom window and sit quietly on the roof, watching the street below. I would wait and wait, not knowing who I was waiting for. During one regression, the truth surfaced. I had been waiting for Thomas.

After my sessions with Judith, once I felt a sense of peace settle into my thoughts and body, I reached out to him. He already knew about my Past Life Regression work and had begun his own spiritual journey. There was a quiet understanding between us, a recognition that didn't need explanation.

After my last session with Judith, I wrote to him:

> "Dear Thomas,
> I will always be here for you in some way or another. I know we've been connected for many years in this lifetime, but it's been quite different from our past lives together... so far apart, yet always spiritually entwined. After doing the regression work that allowed me to see everything clearly, I realized that part of my soul's journey was to find you again to resolve the guilt and heartbreak of losing you.
>
> During my sessions, I felt everything we had shared in that lifetime, and it was so hard to let go. I wasn't ready... I didn't want to. But now, in this life, I have no place in your day-to-day world, except to remain in the background as a quiet companion to your spirit. I found you. I've seen the truth behind the overwhelming loss I've carried for so long. To try and keep that past life alive, even in my mind, would dishonor its purpose, diminish the healing it offered, and distract me from the tasks I am meant to fulfill in this lifetime."

Remembering the loss of him and feeling the release of pain from my heart gave me a sense of peace I hadn't known before. I know now that we will always be connected spiritually, and that we will meet again in the space between this life and the next. I strive to see myself through his eyes, the way he always saw me... with love, with grace. I feel whole in the memory of him because I was loved by him. And that love will never leave me. It is part of who I am.

During my healing process, I was able to mourn and move on. I noticed that my arm had stopped hurting and that I no longer experienced the eye twitch. I was now open to new relationships because of my awareness of the patterns I had developed when faced with the pain of loss and self-survival. Throughout this process, I was able to recognize how healing can take place when one chooses to let go and honor the past without needing to relive it. Like my mother, I hold close to our family history and honor her past as well as my own. Struggle and harmony balance our lives, and we are eternally entwined within the multigenerational history of our families. I strive to integrate my mother's sense of love and loyalty. Now I can choose how I manifest these qualities in my own life.

For years, I had been haunted by guilt, unable to recognize when others were not truly available for love or commitment. I blamed myself for entering relationships that cycled between hope and heartbreak. My shame ran deep. How could I be so knowledgeable about mental health and still miss the truth in my own life? How could I presume to help others? That question became part of my healing. It reminded me that wisdom is not perfection; it is the willingness to see, to feel, to grow.

Charlene's Insight Years Later

It has been many years since my PLRH, and I look back with the perspective of time. I realized the story was not so much about Thomas as it was about me and my feeling of self-worth. It was about seeing myself through his eyes, as he often told me he wished I could. Of being loved for who I was and now who I am.

My dilemma was very reminiscent of Ana (Chapter 6), feeling that she was only valuable through service and sacrifice. I utilize my experience of spiritual healing and the release of pain as an inspiration for me to continue growing and to be present in every moment of everyday life.

With the newly acquired knowledge from the depths of my subconscious, I feel equipped to move forward through whatever tragedies or disasters present themselves. I know that this life is but a delicate string of moments sewn together, and it continues well beyond this lifetime. We will pass on to our beloved future generations a tapestry of our lives that is woven with resilience, love, and the stories that shaped us.

Reader Takeaway

Charlene had spent her life feeling that there was something missing. She was diagnosed with depression and anxiety and prescribed appropriate medication. Yet neither the medication nor psychotherapy relieved her symptoms or eased her insomnia. After undergoing hypnotherapy, she gradually improved. She was sleeping through the night and discovering a renewed sense of energy and hope for the future.

Like Carl (Chapter 3), Charlene struggled to find meaning in her loss. Also, like Carl, once she understood the root of her attachment to Thomas, she was able to find meaning in a life without him. She was also, again like Carl, able to forgive Thomas for leaving, and forgiveness is a major tool for healing. Unresolved grief is maintained by uncertainty, and once the picture is complete, no matter how dire, the clarity provides the impetus for healing and a path forward. The work of Pauline Boss (2006) on ambiguous loss provides a clear rationale for the importance of coming to terms with the reality of the situation and acting accordingly. This allows for integrity in relationships, rather than living and relating "as if...." This work is critical in the case of unresolved grief whether it was caused by death, departure, or lack of resolution.

Chapter 10

Voices Within and Threats Without

When the mind fractures under unbearable fear,
its visions may be woven from many places at once.
Memory, imagination, trauma, and terror.
In psychosis, past and present blur until every shadow feels real.
Healing begins when even the most frightening visions are witnessed with compassion rather than judgment.

Author

Jorge's story was one of profound confusion, both for him and for those trying to help him. Diagnosed with substance use disorder as a teenager and then schizophrenia at age 16, now at 19, he lived in a world where the boundaries between inner terror and external threat had eroded. He had failed out of high school and had never been able to keep even the most menial of jobs.

His mother, Elena, had spent many years oscillating between fear, frustration, and helplessness. Jorge was a gifted painter, but his paintings terrified her. They also terrified her friends and potential clients who refused to pay for portraits that they had ordered from him.

Jorge's experience occurred against the backdrop of Apartheid in South Africa. He and his friends and classmates grew up on the wrong side of the "color barrier," which meant frequent imprisonment for not carrying their "book of life" or "passbook." Others were taken in the night, never to be seen again.

Jorge was convinced that he was on a "list of those to be caught and killed," but couldn't explain what the list was, who was keeping it, or where it might be found. He just knew that one night, he would be taken and never seen or heard from again. In between his rants of evil doers, he was, in his mother's words, "My own sweet son for a moment.... then this stranger appears...."

DOI: 10.4324/9781003636182-11

Many nights, Elena would be woken by the sounds of Jorge's demonic laughter, which she said, "Made my blood run cold." On other occasions, he would climb into her bed sobbing like a little boy, clinging to her as though his life depended on never letting her go.

She was exhausted and terrified that she was losing her son one day at a time. He refused to take any prescribed medication, convinced that the psychiatrist was planning to kill him.

Jorge had attended a day care program for a short while, but the staff was unable to care for him because of his unpredictable moods and intermittent aggression. He was also prone to getting into vicious arguments and occasional fights with the other young men attending the program. Elena was at her wits' end.

When one of Elena's friends had an exciting consultation with a Past Life Regression Hypnotherapist, the possibility that this type of therapy might reveal the roots of Jorge's paranoia offered her a rare kind of hope; the hope that meaning might exist beneath the chaos.

During the time of my work with Jorge, I was studying with a very experienced child psychiatrist and training Jungian analyst (Dr. Vera Bührmann, who had studied with Carl Jung in Zurich). My goal was to learn from her how to work with youth dealing with autism and schizophrenia.

Jorge was one of the young people attending the day clinic in which I was doing my residency. Many of the youth at the clinic, like Jorge, were also using large amounts of THC (Marijuana or Dagga as it was called in Cape Town at the time) to try to manage their psychotic symptoms. The result for some was to extend their psychosis and for many who had never been psychotic, precipitate psychosis for the first time.

When I asked Vera whether I could use hypnotherapy with Jorge, she gave me her blessing and said that it couldn't do any harm. She also gave me permission to include his mother in the therapy sessions, something which in those days was highly unusual. The nurses and social workers "saw" the mothers while the child psychiatrist worked with the children. The concept of family therapy was in its infancy and was not yet accepted as a legitimate form of psychotherapy.

It was on one of my home visits, again not part of the clinic routine in those days, that I was able to see Jorge's paintings and began to understand his mother's fears for his sanity. His artistic ventures ranged from the beautiful faces of women to those of demons and horror. Sometimes it was a combination of the two, a beautiful woman with demonic, emerald green eyes and a menacing smile. Grimacing snakes began to replace her gorgeous golden tresses. Another painting was of a beautiful young boy, but crocodiles and lions emerged from a cavernous mouth with tool-like teeth.

As a young Past Life Regression Hypnotherapist, this was going to be an exciting challenge, and I understood that I would need to move forward very cautiously. It was only after several visits (both in his home and in my office) that Jorge, his mother, and I all felt that he was ready to proceed.

Jorge's Story

When Judith told me to close my eyes, I thought I was going to fall apart. But then everything got dark... not scary dark, just empty. Like when I used to hide in the storage closet at school so nobody could find me. Suddenly, I wasn't in her room anymore. I was running. Running down an alleyway. It was night, and I could feel people chasing me. They were yelling in some language I didn't know. I was clutching my paintings to my chest. My hands were shaking. I kept saying to myself,

"If they take my paintings, they'll take my mind, too."

I suddenly became aware of my mother's voice saying,

"When he says that I can feel my stomach twist. He always used to scream that people were trying to take his thoughts. I never knew where it came from. Hearing him describe it now.... it's like listening to an echo I've lived with for years. I find it terrifying!"

It was horrible hearing my mother talk about me like that and I could feel the tears coming.

Judith said, *"Go to the next significant moment,"* and counted, *"one... two...three...click."*

I suddenly saw myself from above, like I was floating. I saw myself.

"I am just a kid, maybe thirteen. Thin. Hungry. Terrified. My paintings were wrapped in cloth of bright colors... blues, reds, and golds. They look like my visions. The kind I can't talk about. The kind that get you killed. I can't be here anymore...."

During our debriefing meeting with Judith the following week, my mother started to talk about me as if I wasn't there.

"For two days he was calm. He slept. He let me bring him soup. He said the voices were quieter. Then on the third day they came back, soft, not screaming, and for the first time, he told me, he said, 'They're far away today, Mama. Like they're tired.'"

It was strange hearing her talk about me with me sitting right there next to her. I said,

"I wasn't scared the same way this time. Something about seeing that boy... seeing myself... made the voices feel like memories instead of like monsters."

I agreed to try taking the medication again. I felt that I could trust that Judith wasn't trying to kill me. I made her promise that I could stop if they felt bad again.

While we waited for our second session, I was able to paint some of my thoughts to share with Judith and my mother. One of the paintings was of

Judith, and I wanted to give it to her. But I was worried that my mother would think it would frighten her away because my paintings often frightened people. I decided to wait and give it to her later when I knew that she was going to see me again.

Our next session was to be another hypnotherapy session because Judith said that I was ready because I had done very well with our debriefing and my journal writing. When she counted down again from 10 to 1, it was like falling into warm sand. I saw a room. The walls were stone. I was older this time, maybe in my twenties. I was painting on wood. Not paper. Wood. And people were waiting outside the door.

I remember thinking, "If they see what I'm painting, I'll die. I keep hearing drums outside. It's the same sound I hear in my head sometimes. They're not drums in real life. They're footsteps. Footsteps coming to get me!"

And then... Mama walked into the room. Not her, but someone who felt like her. She was scared, too. She wrapped her arms around me and said,

"Hide your mind. Hide your visions so they don't come and get you!"

I hear my mother crying, and she said, "I don't know why I'm crying. It feels like something from long ago is breaking inside me."

At the next debriefing session with Judith, my mother said,

"He was softer this past week. He let me open the curtains. He let me wash his clothes. He came out of the house on the fourth day and sat in the sun for twenty minutes. That hadn't happened in months."

Once again, it felt strange hearing my mother talk about me as I sat there. But her words were kind, and I didn't mind much. I told Judith and my mother that I still hear things. I still feel I am being watched. But there is this new feeling, too, like something isn't chasing me anymore.

At our third hypnotherapy session, I saw myself as much older... maybe in my forties. I was blind in one eye. My hands were stained with paint that wouldn't wash off. People came to me secretly to ask for visions. Through my paintings, people knew that I had a gift. Then the king's guards came. They dragged me out of the house. They burned my paintings. They said I was dangerous. That I stole the visions from God.

My mother said,

"When he says they burned his artwork, I feel like I'm swallowing fire. All those years of trying to convince him no one wanted his paintings... and here is the truth. I have been arguing with a ghost. I couldn't win."

I thought about this and said, "Despite what my mother is saying, I don't feel crazy. In this moment. I feel... understood. Like I finally know why the world felt so dangerous."

In our final debriefing, my mother told Judith, "Since agreeing to take medication after that first session he has been much better. He even said to me, 'Maybe it's time I stop running.' I almost fainted. I'd been begging him for years. But something shifted. He didn't talk about losing his creativity. He talked about wanting peace."

I told my mother, "After these sessions with Judith, I just didn't want to live like that anymore. I didn't want to keep thinking everyone could hear my thoughts. I didn't want to hide in my room. The visions had meaning.... they didn't disappear, but they stopped chasing me."

Reader Takeaway

Jorge's hypnotherapy sessions did not cure his psychosis, nor did they replace the need for medication or clinical care. Instead, they revealed the emotional and symbolic roots of his terror. What unfolded over the course of several sessions was a tapestry of memories, fear, and finally a level of clarity that allowed both mother and son to understand what had remained hidden for too long.

By providing narrative form to his fear, witnessed by his mother and not him alone, and by allowing him to see that his overwhelming paranoia was the echo of persecution in both this and another lifetime, he found a way to separate historical trauma from present reality (van der Kolk, 2014; Walsh & McGoldrick, 1991).

Unlike Charlotte (Chapter 1), who had been diagnosed with having psychosis and possibly schizophrenia because of her hallucinations, Jorge's diagnosis was not in question. However, for both, discovering the links to their past was a powerful facilitator for healing. By exploring their histories both in this lifetime and in earlier ones, real or metaphoric, it allowed for clarity of diagnosis and helped with the direction of treatment (American Psychiatric Association, 2022).

The integration of regression work with clinical stabilization allowed him not merely to function, but to reclaim the creative life he had been too terrified to inhabit. Regression-based approaches, when used as an adjunct with clinical care, can support meaning and emotional integration (Weiss, 1988). This mirrors broader trauma frameworks emphasizing stabilization before deeper processing (Herman, 2015).

Chapter 11

The Lion Within

The instinct to protect,
The pain of loss,
The devotion to family:
These are not uniquely human
They are older than any species and stronger than time

Author

Introduction and Background

Andrew, a successful businessman with a sharp mind and a well-ordered life, had always been a man of logic. He prided himself on being in control of his life, his schedule, his finances, and his emotions. He had always organized his life the way a mathematician arranges numbers: cleanly, sensibly, and predictably. His colleagues admired his brilliance; his friends admired his loyalty; his wife admired his steadiness. The shift in his life had begun a decade ago during a perfectly planned family trip to Southern Africa. Something ancient stirred within him, something that shattered his illusion of control and led him down a path he had never expected.

At first, he dismissed it as travel fatigue. Then a unique dream sequence interrupted his sleep and his daytime concentration. "I couldn't remember them when I woke up," Andrew shared with his family and me at our first meeting, his voice low with an uneasiness apparently unusual for him. "I couldn't remember the details when I woke up. No clear pictures. But I knew, without question, that I was dreaming the *same* dream repeatedly. The same scent. The same sense of loss. The same fear. The same evasive scent. The same urgency. I'd awaken drenched in sweat, heart racing, and with an uneasy feeling, a deep ache that would follow me throughout the day."

His wife, Rachel, explained that she had noticed the change in Andrew immediately upon their return from Africa. Andrew, usually attentive and grounded, had become distracted and distant. Their sons, Ben (11) and

DOI: 10.4324/9781003636182-12

Lucas (9), had asked both parents why Dad was so quiet. Andrew couldn't explain it. He only knew that the dream was growing stronger and more frequent as he became more exhausted and distracted. But it wasn't an illness. It was a memory.

Then came the lions. On the second day of their safari, Andrew had felt an overwhelming pull toward a lioness and her cubs resting in the tall grass. Without thinking, he had stepped toward them, as if drawn by an invisible thread. Rachel had screamed, grabbed his arm, and yanked him back so abruptly that he stumbled into her. Andrew wasn't in the least afraid. He was overcome by a feeling of recognition so deep that he described it as sacred. This unexpected feeling of kinship with the lions was so powerful that he moved enthusiastically toward a large lioness and her cubs without realizing any possible danger. He was offended by Rachel's move to pull him back, not because she had removed him from danger, but because she had stopped him from approaching what he felt to be his family. "I knew her," he told me. "It wasn't logical. I just knew the lioness and her cubs."

His feelings of connection to the lions intensified after they returned home. So did the dreams. Andrew couldn't shake the feelings of being part of the lioness' family. The longing to return to Southern Africa and the lions intensified. He began researching Past Life Regression Hypnotherapy (PLRH), hoping to find a thread that might explain the visceral ache now woven through his days. That search led him to my office. And it led him back to a lifetime he had never imagined.

Andrew's Story

Judith's office was warm and quiet, filled with soft light and the scent of lavender. I sat across from her, nervous but determined. My wife sat in a comfortable chair nearby. "I don't know what I'm looking for, but I know something's trying to reach me." Then I told Judith about our family trip to Southern Africa. "It wasn't just curiosity that drove me to travel there, but a need. I knew that in some profound way, I had a connection to that continent and that something about it was drawing me to it."

Judith asked us all to find our 'Place of Joy,' a place where we would feel safe and peaceful and where nothing bad could touch us. My sons both chose our quiet backyard, where they spent many hours climbing our large oak tree. I had helped them build a tree house, and that was their favorite place for retreat.

Rachel described her experience of finding herself next to a beautiful pond surrounded by wildflowers with the sound of birdsong. "Before I was to share my 'Place of Joy,' I was already in the African bush, in a quiet clearing safe from predators and hunters. It was not a real spot I had visited before. Something older. A clearing where the grass whispered like breath. Warm wind. Wide sky. A place that felt like memory, not imagination."

Judith told us she would work mostly with me during the first session, but that Rachel and the boys were free to come along in whatever way felt natural. Little did we realize then how intertwined our journeys would become. She invited them to relax and join the hypnotherapy. They were to observe and, if they found themselves in the scene with me, were free to participate.

Judith guided us all toward a deep relaxation, using breathwork and visualization to help us relax. She then suggested that I go to my 'Place of Joy' as she counted from 1 to 10. As my body relaxed, my mind opened. Images began to surface: dusty plains, sun-heated grass, and something wilder, animal musk in golden fur, the weight of an overwhelming responsibility.

"I'm... lower to the ground," I remember saying. "Everything is sharper. I can hear insects from yards away. A branch snapping far in the distance. I can feel every movement." And then it hit me like a truth I'd always known. "I'm not a man, I'm... I'm a lioness." The words came out before I thought them. My whole body reacted. It wasn't symbolic. It wasn't a dream. It was a *memory*.

I'm watching over my pride. I feel everything. Every movement. I hear every sound. I'm responsible for the survival of everyone! Every cub, every vulnerable body, depending on me! The fear, the vigilance, the hyper-awareness... it all felt familiar. Too familiar.

Then the grief arrived. Tears streamed down my face as my panic grew. "One of my cubs is missing. I can't find her. I smell blood. I've failed. I've failed her."

Judith gently encouraged me to stay with the feeling, to honor it without judgment. She told me to rise above the scene, to look without feeling the full force of the pain. From that vantage point, I saw it clearly.

"I know I should have been watching my cub more closely. She was the curious one. There is one in every litter. She always wanted to explore. She must have wandered too far. I should have been watching. I knew there were jackals and hyenas nearby. She wouldn't have stood a chance. She was so little and defenseless. I should have moved faster! I should have known! In the depths of my soul, I did know that she had been killed."

My body was trembling. My grief was raw, both present and ancient, and real. I broke down. My whole body shook. And suddenly, my grief as a lioness collided with my grief as a father. The ache that had lived in me for years when I lost my daughter surged through me again. I realized, "I've carried this since that lifetime. I just didn't know until now." Rachel's hand was in mine. Rachel grabbed my hand, crying with me. She later told me that hearing me call myself a lioness made something ancient in her chest crack open, too. She said that she really understood why I had been drawn to the lioness, and she also felt my loss keenly as though one of our own children had been taken.

We both found ourselves sobbing with the vivid, overwhelming memory of the loss of our firstborn daughter. She had been born with a serious heart abnormality and had died during reparative surgery at the age of nine days. As we sobbed, our sons clung to us. They had not known that there was a big sister long before they were born. It had taken us six years to have the courage to become pregnant again, and we had seen no reason to share the heartbreaking story with our boys.

Judith had asked us to journal after each session. Our sons chose to do drawings, and Rachel and I decided to keep them for their future amusement. My pages were filled with emotion, memory, and revelation. During our first debriefing session, I explained to Judith and my family, "I understand now why I've always needed to know where my family is. Why do I panic when I can't reach Rachel or the boys. It's not just anxiety. It's instinct. It's the lioness in me. It's my commitment never to lose another cub."

Judith asked me to track my emotional responses and notice when the lioness energy surged.

Was it at airports, in crowded places, or during moments of separation? She and Rachel helped me create rituals to soothe my instinct: grounding breathwork, affirmations of safety, and visualizations of my family surrounded by white light. I would say to myself, "I am no longer in the wild. My family is safe. I can rest."

During our second hypnotherapy session (our third meeting), Judith once again guided all of us through the progressive relaxation exercise and invited us to return to our 'Places of Joy.'

What do you see, smell, feel, hear? ...1 ...2...3 ...click

I didn't *just* ease in, I fell. "I smell rain. And blood." And, as the trance deepened, I said, "My cub is dying." Rachel gasped beside me, and I could feel her fear and compassion. "Rain, blood, and fur sticky with blood. My cub is injured. She is dying...I can't save her!" I felt the pain of the moment in vivid detail, the chase, the confusion, the helplessness. Judith asked me, "*Let yourself float out of your body and observe from above where you can see and hear everything that happens, but you won't feel the pain.*" "I wasn't fast enough. I wasn't strong enough. I have failed her."

Again, Judith guided me to float above myself. From that higher view, I saw what I hadn't seen in the first session: I hadn't failed my cub. I had been protecting the rest of the pride. I couldn't abandon them, or they all would've been in danger. That realization opened something inside me, in a good way.

Once I was back in the room and feeling calm, Judith asked me to speak to myself, the lioness. "*What would you say to her now?*" I asked: "You did your best. You loved her. You protected her as best you could. You had responsibility for the others, the entire pride. You couldn't leave them to search for the missing one in case you lost them all. You were not meant to control everything. It is never possible."

The room was silent. A shift occurred. "I've never forgiven myself for the loss of our daughter. Why didn't I know there was something wrong during the pregnancy. Why did my intuition fail me. It's my job to protect my family, my loved ones." As I said this, I realized how impossible a task I had set myself. I realized that maybe it's time for me to forgive myself for the loss of my daughter and for my lion cub.

"I've never forgiven myself for our daughter's death," I admitted. "But I couldn't have saved her. I now understand that I wasn't supposed to. I see how impossible it was to change a congenital abnormality." Rachel, the boys, and I all cried together, and at that moment, something healed in both of us, quietly but deeply.

At the next hypnotherapy session, Session 3, Rachel went from her quiet pond to a dramatic scene. I don't think either of us expected what happened. "I'm in tall grass," she said. "My body is huge. I'm a lion. A male." I remember the boys staring at her, wide-eyed.

"There are hunters," she said. "Warriors from some other tribes are circling. They're searching for me."

"No one sees me as I crawl slowly through the thick brush. I'm approaching someone. He's turning towards me... he is very young. His eyes widen and his face distorts with fear. I pounce. I feel the brush along my fur, the power of my nails cutting through his skin. I feel tension in my jaw as I ready for the kill..." She jolted out of trance with a gasp, trembling. I held her while Judith kept quietly reassuring her that she was safe.

Rachel didn't want to return to that lifetime, but she said she finally understood why my connection to lions felt sacred. She had been one too, just in a different form, in a different story. We were stunned that both of us had been lions... me female, Rachel male. We didn't know what to make of it. Judith then offered to regress us together, but Rachel did not want to go back into that lifetime. However, she was grateful for the glimpse she had experienced of being a member of a different species, especially one that meant so much to me. The boys were fascinated by the stories and made us promise to take them to the bush in Africa as soon as we could. We explained that it would be several years before it was possible, but we promised that it would happen.

None of us expected that one of our boys was carrying a memory as well.

In Session 4, Lucas entered the story. He came to Judith quietly. "Can I try?" he asked. "I think I remember things." Rachel and I were surprised, but Judith assured us that children sometimes access past life imagery even more easily than adults.

As soon as he relaxed and entered a hypnotic state, he smiled. "I'm small. My paws are tiny."

Judith asked, "Are you an animal?" "Yes! I'm a cub. A lion cub." My breath caught. My son had also been an animal... a lion? He continued, "I'm playing with another cub, and I am little. I am exploring too far away. I hear Mama calling and she is scared."

Rachel covered her mouth. Lucas's expression softened, "I wasn't the one who died. But I remember Mama crying." Tears streamed down my face. My son, my little boy, was remembering a lifetime where he had been one of my cubs. Then, with his eyes still half-closed, he said, "It's okay now. We're all together again." It was amazing. Those words healed something in me that nothing else ever had.

After hearing Lucas share his experience, Ben – who is usually skeptical and logical like I am – said he didn't believe he'd remember anything, but he wanted to try. "I'll just help the others," he said. But halfway through the relaxation, he shifted. "I see shadows," he murmured. "Big ones. I'm supposed to protect everyone. I'm not strong enough yet, but I'm trying."

Rachel placed her hand on his knee. "I'm a young male lion," he continued. "I stay close to the pride because I'm not big enough to fight yet. But I follow our mother lioness everywhere. I watch her. I make sure she's safe." "*Is the lioness important to you?*" Judith asked. "Yes," Ben said simply. "She's family."

I nearly broke down. When he came out of the trance, he looked embarrassed but proud. "That was weird. But... kind of cool." He had been protecting me in another life. And here he was, doing it again in this one, just in a different way.

As our hypnotherapy sessions continued, Rachel talked about how I had begun to change. She had noticed that I had stopped checking our sons' locations every hour. I was also comfortable with Rachel going on a weekend retreat and no longer called her twice a day throughout her absence. The old panic, the lioness, began to release its grip. I noticed that for the first time in many years, I was sleeping through the night.

"I feel lighter," I told Judith. "Not because I've forgotten, but because I've remembered." Rachel and I began volunteering at an animal sanctuary, drawn to the lions but also to the rhythm of caretaking, connection, and trust. We spoke at a local wellness event about the human-animal bond, sharing our stories with vulnerability and integrity. We spoke about our experience not as experts but as a family who had traveled across lifetimes together. "Family isn't just blood," we said. "It's soul. And sometimes, it's fur."

"Family doesn't always stay in the same form," I said. "Sometimes we find each other again as humans. Sometimes as lions." But we find each other. We always do. I used to think success was about control. Now I know it's about connection. I've lived as a lioness. I've grieved as a father. I've healed as a man. And through it all, love is the constant.

Reader Takeaway

Andrew's regression was a profound healing story of soul-level memory and emotional restoration. His vivid recall, the emotional accuracy, and the transformation woven into his daily life revealed more than an intriguing past; it revealed ancestral healing. He didn't just remember, he integrated what was revealed to him. That's the power of soul work that PLRH offers.

Andrew discovered the origin of his deep yearning for closeness, constant physical touching, and continuous awareness of the whereabouts of his family members. He understood that this level of security was not needed to ensure that his human family was safe. He started to understand that it was not only out of reach in his present lifetime, but that it was no longer needed or appropriate. He learned the origin of the fierce, instinctive protection he carried into his fatherhood. He recognized that the vigilance once needed for survival in a lion's world was no longer required in this one.

Rachel's unexpected glimpse into her lion incarnation deepened her understanding of Andrew's experience, allowing her to empathize not only with his past life trauma but with his present-life struggles.

Their sons, through their brief and authentic connections to past life imagery, helped reveal the full picture: a pride reunited, each soul playing a role across time.

Both Andrew and Rachel's experiences remind us that healing is not linear. It's layered, ancestral, and often beyond logic. Their journeys show that the bonds we form, whether human or animal, leave imprints on the soul and on our intergenerational patterns. And sometimes, the path to peace begins with remembering who we were once before. This family's journey into the past gives the reader a wider view and understanding of the strength family connection provides and the devastation if it is lost.

Humans have long questioned the human-animal connection and its benefits, as well as its possible detriments. This chapter shows how the family bond can be found across all species and how intense family connections can cross lifetimes, no matter the form our souls take. Research has shown that the animal-human bond is a strong source of healing energy. Numerous types of animal-assisted therapies exist, ranging from therapy dogs visiting cancer centers to equine therapy for trauma, and canine companions for veterans dealing with post-traumatic stress and/or depression (Jones et al., 2019; Kamioka et al., 2014; Maujean et al., 2015). Research has also shown us that our resilience lies in our connectedness to our family and culture of origin, whatever that may be (Landau, 2018).

Chapter 12

The Thread That Never Breaks

The uncut thread between kindred souls

Author

Ruth is the daughter of German Jewish refugees. She grew up knowing all the family stories, both positive and negative. She led a 'charmed life,' and her self-confidence, her many successes, and her light-heartedness caused many to remark that she was just like her father. At the age of 14, she started suffering from severe depression which she hid from everyone. When possible, she went into her own world to avoid dealing with adults and classmates.

Ruth felt her father was the only person she could trust. They confided in each other; he was her mentor, and for over 40 years, they never had a disagreement. When he died suddenly, she was at a loss. Ruth, diagnosed with bipolar disease, had tried several types of therapy when she was in crisis. Now she felt that she knew exactly what to do. She needed Past Life Regression Hypnotherapy (PLRH). She felt that she and her father had been together many times before, and she needed to know not only about the past, but also if there was a chance that they would meet again in this lifetime or another.

Ruth's Story

I first met Dr. Landau at a reception at the University, where she was the chair of a department at the medical school. We had started talking when a woman came over and began giving me the first few pages of Dr. Landau's very long curriculum vitae (academic biography). What caught my attention was that Dr. Landau practiced PLRH.

I had grown up believing that I had lived many lifetimes before this one. As a young child, I tried to explain to my parents that our bodies were temporary and that when they no longer worked, we still existed in some

DOI: 10.4324/9781003636182-13

other form. We just disappeared for a while. I couldn't believe that energy just dissipated into the ether. My belief was reinforced because I found that I knew my way around places where I had never been before, and I would look into people's eyes and just feel I knew them from other lifetimes. Most importantly, everything about my father felt as though it was a continuation of my past experiences.

I arranged to meet Dr. Landau, Judith, for an initial consult, and at that time we talked about my family history. I did not hold back and told her everything I could think of, including what life was like for both sides of my family as Jews in Germany before and after 1933. How they went from upper middle class to being interned, killed, or becoming refugees. I told her about current family relationships, my medical history, and that there were times when I saw myself floating above a scene, just observing it, while trying to avoid the situation that was happening below me.

However, the most important thing that I talked about was how critical it was for me to find out how I had known my father before and what our lives were like then. I also wanted to know where he was now. Was he floating around somewhere, or was he already in some other "body?" I told Judith, "I am still very angry and upset that he 'left' me." I told her, "He called me on Sunday morning two days before we were supposed to go abroad together on a business trip. He said that on the previous Friday night, he had collapsed in the street and cracked his head. He had to go to the emergency room for stitches the next morning." He said, "I told your mother and sister that I was mugged by some kid, so they don't know the truth about my blacking out. I don't want them to worry about me." Then he asked me, "Do you mind traveling with someone whose face is all mushed up?"

We laughed together about that. Then he reminded me about where he kept his instructions for the family, his financial information, and most importantly, his "private papers" just in case I needed them in the future.

"You're trusting me with all this, Dad?" We both laughed again, knowing that he couldn't trust anyone else in the family. A few jokes later, we hung up because he said he had a lot of phone calls to make.

That Sunday night, from a thousand miles away, I felt that something was terribly wrong. Then my mother called me and said she was driving behind an ambulance taking Dad to the hospital. For several minutes, I felt his presence with me. I was willing him to live. Then everything went blank.

It was a cold day when I arrived at Judith's home office for my first meeting with her. She greeted me so warmly that I started to settle in with a sense of relief. This was finally going to happen.

Judith explained the way she did hypnotherapy. Being in a light trance meant I would always know what was happening and that she would be with me and ready to help me get out of difficult situations. We would debrief at the end of each session, and she wanted me to keep a journal so we could talk about my thoughts and feelings in between sessions. Of course, being who I was, I had to tell her that I really wanted to do this, but I honestly didn't feel that I could be hypnotized.

Our first hypnotherapy session began several days later. Judith repeated the basics and gave me some relaxation suggestions. A good idea, as I was starting to tense up with excitement. She said she would count down from ten to one. As this was happening, she said,

> *I want you to go to a 'Place of Joy.' Some place where you feel safe and happy. A place that might be familiar or that you've hoped would exist. Maybe it is lying down on the ground in a forest or walking down a garden path. Maybe you're on a beach, or in the water. What is most important is that you will be able to return to this place whenever you want to or need to.*

My mind jumped from one place to another as I tried out several possibilities. Then I had it. "I am riding up a ski lift in the early morning. There is fresh, light snow below me and sparkling crystals in the air. The sun is rising to my left, and the moon is setting to my right. I am on a mountain, my sacred place. The lift stops, I close my eyes, and I know this is perfection."

Judith let me stay in this place for a little while. I breathed deeply and I knew I was smiling. She asked me to move on to the next significant place and time, and I heard,

> *one...two...three... click." "Look down at your feet and tell me what you see.*

I looked down and said, "I see very large white furry paws." There is a pause.

> *What do you smell or feel; do you see anything else?*

Everything was very clear. "The smell is awful, I am shoved up against white fur in a cramped place, I just have to get out of here!" I pushed my way out, and the sun was shining; it was warm. I stretched. Much better.

> *What do you see now? What are you?*

I looked around and saw other small, white furries tumble out of a den. I said to Judith, "This is great! I'm a polar bear, and these are my sibs."

We started running around, and then our mother bear came out, and we headed out to find food. Judith said,

Can you jump ahead and tell me what is happening?

At first, I saw us all playing. My brother and I practiced attacking each other while we shoved our sister around. I saw our mother teaching us how to find food and hunt. Then my sister and mother disappeared and were not part of my life anymore. However, while I knew it wasn't normal bear behavior, my brother and I were inseparable.

Judith said to move forward in time, and she snapped her fingers. Something was wrong.

"My brother fell off a ledge into the water," I cried. "No one is helping him. He's drowning. I feel afraid, but I must do something."

I saw myself jump into the water, and I shoved him up on some ice.

Judith let me rest, and then said,

Do you recognize your brother? Look closely.

I looked and exclaimed, "It's Dad! I saved Dad from drowning!" I hugged my current brother and future father. I was so relieved!

When Judith started to bring me back into the present, I was emotionally and physically exhausted. We sat together and I drank some water. I forgot whether it was normal to debrief immediately. Maybe I was supposed to wait, journal, and talk about my feelings and insights at the next session, but I just couldn't wait. It was all so obvious to me, and I had to fill her in.

I started by saying, "I have always loved bears. Some have said that they are my 'Spirit Animal.' As a teenager, I went to a zoo and spent an hour with a very clever polar bear. He had an empty beer keg in his enclosure. A few people joined me and the bear looked over, checked us out, and flipped the keg into the water. He kept trying to get the keg out of the water. He made every maneuver possible, and as he did this, the crowd started to grow. Some yelled advice while others contorted their bodies as if that would help.

After about fifteen minutes, I could start to feel a restlessness in the crowd of about 30 people. The bear felt this too and with a big swat of his paw, he sent the keg flying out of the water. The crowd cheered, laughed, and applauded. Then they left. After a few minutes, the bear looked over as some new people arrived at his enclosure. He flipped the keg into the water, and the show started all over again." I remembered roaring with laughter, and the bear looked over. I couldn't say that he smiled, but I felt we both understood that this was exactly what I would have done.

Forty years later, I was in Churchill, Manitoba, and spent a week out on the Tundra to see polar bears. I told Judith how amazing this was, and how I felt I could die happy having been with these friends. Everything they did was familiar. Sibs played together, and larger bears fought, drew blood, and then walked away together like best friends.

The most important part of my PLRH session was saving my brother bear, my father, from drowning. In this lifetime, my father was deathly afraid of drowning. He had never learned to swim. In January 1942, he crossed the Atlantic in a tiny freighter, and they lost their convoy the first night out. For five weeks, they avoided U-boats as they crisscrossed the Atlantic on their way to New York. Throughout that terrifying trip, he wore a life vest and had his few valuables strapped to himself. His greatest fear was that of drowning.

I told Judith how Dad would never go into water that was deeper than his waist. However, when he was with me, everything was different. He would first get wet up to his shoulders and then stick his face under the water to blow bubbles with me. We'd splash each other and just play. I said to Judith, "I had a very small sailboat that was not particularly stable. One day Dad said he would love to come sailing with me. My mother was shocked."

I went on, "He and I headed to the marina where I put two types of life preservers on him and slipped my 13.5-foot sailboat into the water. There was a slight breeze as we headed out of the harbor. He had not looked happy as we started out, but we talked about all sorts of things, and he relaxed for a little while. He trusted me completely because he knew I would protect him just as I knew he would do the same for me."

Judith asked, "So how was he when you got back to the dock?"

I said, "He got off the boat as quickly as possible. He may have trusted me, but he also said something about not pushing his luck."

I said to him, "Buy me a bigger boat and it will be easier the next time!"

As I left, I told Judith that I could not have been happier with this Past Life Regression session. I said, "I love the cold, I love knowing I was my favorite animal, and I love knowing that such a meaningful relationship had existed with my father and that it carried forward into this lifetime."

A month passed before we could have our next session. When we met again, I was in a very different place. I was depressed and angry. The pressure of having to keep things on an even keel between my mother and sister (which had always been my role and responsibility) had worn me down. Now I felt my meds were not doing their job. Not only had Dad left me to manage these two women, but he also left me with responsibilities to others in his business circle.

Despite my anger and resentment, I explained to Judith, "In all the years we were together we never had a disagreement, and we were either together or in touch several times a week no matter where we were in the world." It was now two years since he died. I asked her, "Why hasn't he come back to visit me and advise me what to do."

Judith went over some of my history with me. We talked about how, even at an early age, there were many times that I felt abandoned by my family and friends. In my mind, Dad was my one constant. Now he was dead, and I felt truly alone. Judith reminded me about all the wonderful and joyful times I had had with my father. She reminded me about my stories and how we found so many things to laugh about. I told her that with all the crazy things that I had done, I never thought I would live past 40.

"Never did I think I would outlive him. Now I am 42, and he is not here with me."

After talking about all of this, I felt ready to do another PLRH session. I felt I needed and wanted to find out so many more things about where I had been and with whom.

Once again, Judith asked me to relax using all the methods we had used before. There was breath awareness, letting go of tension in each limb and every muscle, and clearing my mind. It seemed to take longer for me to relax this time, but a moment later she was guiding me back to my 'Place of Joy.'

This time it was different. I told her,

"I'm floating in the middle of a coral reef. I am weightless. I am seeing and surrounded by the most beautiful fish and coral and there seems to be an octopus that wants to play with me."

It was fabulous. I was glad this was the place I could return to for safety. Judith counted backward from ten and I don't think I heard the last four numbers. I was in my trance and floating.

Judith let me float for a while and then suggested that we move to the next scene. "*One...two...three...click.*" I heard her ask, "*Look down, what do you see? What do you smell and what do you feel?*"

"I'm looking down and I see shiny, high riding boots. I am trying to avoid my horse's hooves. I have hold of a beautiful stallion who is very eager to move out of his enclosure and drink some water." I told Judith that I needed to take care of feeding him first and foremost.

"The sun is hot and there are smells of sweat. Food with exotic spices are cooking a little bit away. I need water and I want to eat."

Judith asked me, "*Do you know who you are and where you are?*"

I look around and see there is a cavalry regiment forming up. I tell her,

"I am young and in the uniform of a Lieutenant, 7th Dragoons of the British Army. We are far from home, and we have been fighting near a Coastline. I don't know where." I add, "We are fighting with the French against the Russians."

Judith interrupted and said, "How do you feel?"

I had to think. I knew we did well in our earlier battles, but I didn't feel good about this next one.

"I think it is the Fall of 1845 because I just had my 21st birthday before leaving home. This magnificent horse was a special birthday present for me. He is strong, willing and gentle for a stallion. We understand each other and I know we love each other. I think our Captain had said after we capture another Port we would go home. I am happy about that."

I was sweating and agitated. There was a lot of shouting. I looked at my men, and while some had the bravado of a Dragoon, others looked as frightened as I was. As I looked across the line, I saw the officers of the High Command. To the side, I saw my Colonel and some others.

The Colonel was my Godfather, and we had spent many happy times together. He was the one who had encouraged me to enter the army. I tell Judith,

"The Colonel is Dad. I must get to him to tell him this is a mistake. But I am frozen in place. I can't move or call out. I realize he can't answer me. I don't know if he even sees me."

I looked again and now he was looking at me. I saw sadness in his face.

"It is like he knows something is wrong and he wants to protect me. He can't."

I thought that as we looked at each other, it was as if we had an understanding that we would see each other again.

The charge started and the noise was deafening. Those around me were getting shot, but I raced on. Then it happened. I paused and Judith said,

What is happening? How do you feel?

"I am burning up. My horse is shot, and he has fallen on top of me crushing my leg. We are both in terrible pain – we are both dying."

I was beside myself in physical and emotional pain. My horse was down. He trusted me, and I could do nothing to get to my gun and put him out of his misery. It was awful and then I heard Judith's reassurance,

Float away from your body and look down at yourself from above. You are not feeling the pain. Your horse understands.

During my final debriefing, the entire picture had become clear to me. My father and I were connected across time and space through many lifetimes. I found that during the regression process, I had slowly forgiven him for leaving me and was feeling grateful that we had been together so many times. I also realized that the chronic pain in my leg was the result of my wonderful horse falling onto me during the battle. After the last regression, the pain was gone.

Reader Takeaway

It was clear from the PLRH that Ruth and her father had been extremely close in every lifetime that they had shared. Throughout their history, their lives were fraught with challenges, both personal and political. They had lost each other time and again, only to find each other once more.

In each of their shared lifetimes, there was a level of intimacy and trust between them that denied the parent-child relationship. They supported one another, regardless of the environment and stood together against the enemy.

Ruth's psychiatric history matched her past life history. It was not surprising that the overwhelming grief and loss was mirrored by her bipolar disease. Her family history was also filled with loss and unresolved grief, and many family members had a history of depression and/or bipolar disease.

Her discoveries during the past life exploration helped her come to terms with the loss of her beloved father. She was able to sleep better and look forward to life in a different way. However, as with many patients dealing with chronic, relapsing diseases, her need for medication and therapy continued concurrently with a significant improvement in her quality of life that she attributed to PLRH (Sullivan et al., 2012; Miklowitz, 2007).

Conclusion

Beyond Remembering: Living with Meaning

This book has followed 12 individuals and their families as they confronted pain, loss, fear, illness, and uncertainty, sometimes rooted in this lifetime, sometimes experienced as reaching far beyond it. Across these chapters, one truth has emerged with increasing clarity: Healing does not require certainty about the past. It requires meaning, witnessing, and relationship in the present.

Whether experienced as literal past lives, symbolic narratives, embodied memory, or metaphor, the material that surfaced during Past Life Regression Hypnotherapy (PLRH) served a single essential function. It gave form to what had previously been unspeakable. Symptoms that once appeared random, frightening, or senseless became intelligible responses to overwhelming loss, loyalty, terror, and love. When suffering was understood rather than judged, healing became possible.

Throughout this book, readers have seen how symptoms, including chronic pain, eating disorders, addiction, psychosis, relational conflict, and complicated grief, were not signs of defect or failure. They were carriers of history. They held memories that had not yet found language, often transmitted across generations through silence, sacrifice, and unresolved mourning. Healing became possible not because the past was proven, but because it was finally witnessed.

A central teaching of this work is that healing is profoundly relational. Insight alone was rarely sufficient. Change occurred when experiences were shared, believed, and held by family members, therapists, and clinical teams working collaboratively. Transformation followed moments of recognition: when a spouse understood the weight of inherited loyalty, when a parent saw a child's symptoms as protection rather than rebellion, when a family acknowledged grief that had shaped generations. PLRH, as presented here, is not a replacement for medical or psychiatric care. Many of the individuals in these chapters lived with serious, chronic, and sometimes life-threatening conditions that required ongoing medication and professional treatment. What regression offered was not cure, but coherence.

DOI: 10.4324/9781003636182-14

It provided a bridge between symptom and story, between body and meaning, between science and spirit. In doing so, it reduced terror, restored agency, and expanded the capacity to live.

By the later chapters of this book, another truth becomes evident: healing does not mean the absence of pain, illness, or grief. Some losses remain irreversible. Some diagnoses remain lifelong. What changes is not the reality of loss, pain, and grief, but the individual's relationship to it. Compulsion gives way to choice. Fear gives way to compassion. Isolation gives way to connection. Life becomes livable again, even when it remains imperfect.

Across these stories, readers have witnessed individuals and families:

- Interrupt patterns rooted in unspoken grief and fear
- Release inherited burdens they did not choose
- Restore voice where silence once protected survival
- Reclaim agency from symptoms that previously dictated their lives
- Choose love and presence where avoidance once prevailed

Beneath each lifetime's struggle lay a deeper thread: the soul's enduring attempt to heal what was left unfinished. Many of the patients were dealing with diagnosable conditions that also required collaborative medical treatment. However, regardless of diagnosis, all found relief at some level through the process of PLRH which can provide an effective bridge between scientific medicine and spiritual healing.

Healing, as shown here, is rarely dramatic or final. It unfolds through moments of insight, courage, and relational repair. It is sustained through collaboration between patient and therapist, between family members, and between experiential and medical approaches. At its core lies the human capacity to remember, not to remain bound to the past, but to move forward with greater freedom.

We saw how pain can echo across generations and lifetimes. It can also be converted from emotional to physical experiences, both spoken, but just as frequently, never mentioned. We also learn that physical pain and chronic illness can be alleviated by collaborative spiritual understanding and clinical care.

- Natalie's chronic pain carried the memory of wounds unspoken.
- Jennifer's suicide resulted from grief and fear of loss, which originated in centuries-old separations and unhealed attachment ruptures. Carl's understanding of her story facilitated his ability to move beyond his own unresolved grief to healing.
- Couples locked in conflict, like Michael and Laura, or wondering whether they should be together, like Pauline and Malcolm, discovered that their relationship was not only interpersonal but intergenerational and inter-lifetime.

- Silent vows of sacrifice, as in Ana's case, persisted as eating disorder, binding the soul to old promises. Ana also shows us the importance of clinical collaborative care in the management of chronic, life-threatening illness.
- Visions, voices, and terror, as in Jorge's story, were not just symptoms of serious mental illness, but also the remnants of trauma too ancient for language. His story is in sharp contrast with Charlotte's, where the process of PLRH enabled her treatment team to have a deeper understanding of what she had endured. The team was also to recognize that she was not dealing with psychosis like that of Jorge.

These individuals were not defective, broken, or beyond help. They were carrying history, and once that history was witnessed and acknowledged, especially by beloved family members, transformation became possible. In many instances, additional or adjunctive and collaborative therapies were needed for healing, but in every case, their past life experiences enriched that healing process. These stories reveal the transformative power of remembering...whether real, imagined, or metaphoric. PLRH is not presented as a replacement for clinical care, but as a companion to it. It is a collaborative method for enhancing our capacity to:

- Uncover the origins of persistent emotional and physical suffering
- Modulate the level of physical and emotional pain
- Integrate unconscious fears into conscious understanding
- Break intergenerational cycles of self-abandonment, addiction, self-harm, triangulation, and shame
- Restore agency and meaning to the present life
- Provide hope for the future

When a story is "remembered," something vital shifts. Patterns that once felt immovable become more flexible. Patients discover new inner landscapes where choice replaces compulsion, and compassion replaces fear and judgment. Once they understand the origin of the unconscious drivers of their behavior, the individuals and their families can make conscious changes for the present and future.

Across each chapter, readers witnessed patients:

- Release inherited burdens
- Dismantle patterns rooted in old wounds
- Choose love where fear once prevailed
- Find their voices after lifetimes of silence
- Envision a future no longer dictated by the past

Healing does not come instantly or neatly. It comes in small moments of recognition, insight, and courage. It comes through the tapestry of collaboration between therapist, patient, and when indicated, the family and clinical team. Most importantly, it comes from the soul's enduring will to survive, evolve, and love again. The stories in this book are not meant to convince, but to invite the reader to explore further.

This book is not meant to persuade or convert. It is an invitation. An invitation to reflect on your own patterns, your family stories, and the meanings your body and emotions may be carrying. You need not believe in past lives to consider that your struggles may have deeper roots, or that compassion toward those roots can loosen their hold. Every step toward understanding is a step toward choice. Every act of witnessing creates the possibility of change.

We invite the reader to consider that:

- Our deepest struggles may have roots beyond this lifetime
- Change is possible even when patterns feel ancient and immutable
- Understanding the past frees the present and allows us to make positive choices about the future, building on our intergenerational resilience rather than being overwhelmed by our intergenerational vulnerability
- Compassion for self and others can repair wounds across generations
- Healing is not linear; nor is it bound by time
- Every step toward remembering is a step toward freedom
- Every new insight brings the potential for resilience, clarity, and meaning

Have you developed clarity about the meaning of your life? Have your beliefs changed in any way? Are you ready to become an advocate for yourself and others? What have you learned about your own life and relationships?

For the professional reader, we encourage you to review not only your own experiences but also to see how you might integrate the theory and technique of this method into your own practice. These patients have taught us a great deal about the interface of traditional healing and modern medicine and how it is sometimes necessary to embrace the ideology of 'both/and' and not be bound to a definitive 'either/or.' We hope that their stories of challenge, trauma, resilience, and healing stimulate your interest and your commitment to collaborative care.

As you close this book, may you carry with you the knowledge that your story did not begin here. But your healing can.

Appendix: Past Life Regression Hypnotherapy: Place of Joy

A Method of Hypnotherapy for Individuals and Families

"There are rivers that run beneath the skin
currents unseen, remembering where we came from.
To touch them is to wake the ancient pulse
that binds the living to the luminous."

Author

"The soul drifts between worlds like a sound without echo,
carrying every life it has ever known.
Healing begins when we listen to its quiet return."

Author

Most people come to Past Life Regression Hypnotherapy with a desire to find answers. They carry questions about lingering experiences, recurring patterns, lost connections, and the deeper meaning of their present life. There is an eagerness, a yearning, to travel through the veils of time and uncover the wisdom that lies hidden in the soul's memory. Others seek relief from intractable pain, acute or recurring depression and anxiety, and other persistent symptoms that are not responding to psychological or medical treatment. Past Life Regression Hypnotherapy can be both rapid and profoundly transformative. It offers not only relief from current and past difficulties but also an awakening to a broader, more spiritual awareness of who we truly are.

Through our own journeys into past life memories, we discovered how revisiting those experiences opened an expanded understanding of ourselves. This discovery inspired us to share the process with our clients. Over time, we have found that the greatest healing emerges from a positive, collaborative approach. Unlike traditional methods that rely on a deep state of hypnosis, our process uses a light level that keeps the client in control, alert, and fully able to access both their memories and their inherent resilience. This light state of hypnotic trance allows complete recollection of the entire experience. The client can vividly access and later revisit memories at will, integrating their insight with ease. Dr. Gerald Gale (2025), an experienced hypnotherapist, refers to this state as "relational meditation," implying that it is a state of mutual collaboration.[1]

We call this hypnotherapy method 'A Place of Joy.' It is founded on partnership and personal choice rather than control. Because public portrayals of hypnosis often provoke anxiety, we begin by dispelling misconceptions. As we often remind our clients, *"Hypnosis is only a form of focused concentration. You never give up control. You are always in charge. All hypnosis is self-hypnosis."* Understanding that hypnosis is simply an enhancement of concentration helps clients relax. They quickly realize that they experience self-hypnosis in everyday life when absorbed in a film, a book, or daydreaming about a future event. Everyone can remember being brought suddenly to the present from a deep state of concentration. Many of us have had the experience of "being on autopilot." A sense of "how did I get here?" after a long drive home. This is a hypnotic state. Once they recognize this familiar state, fear gives way to curiosity and trust. Krasner's description of clinical hypnotherapy provides a graphic picture of the standard form.

Regression hypnotherapy may bring up deep emotional material. Establishing a 'Place of Joy' during the very first session provides a sanctuary of safety and calm. It becomes a refuge the clients can return to whenever emotions run high. Each person's sanctuary is unique: a landscape of peace, beauty, love, and renewal. It may be drawn from real life or imagination and can be used both in session and in daily living. Once the client knows they can retreat there at any time, they become more confident in facing whatever arises. We practice entering and leaving this place until it becomes second nature.

One client shared afterward, "The whole process was far less intrusive than I had imagined. I felt safe. The feeling of absolute peace, beauty and truth has stayed with me and was such a pleasant surprise. I had been braced for tension and pain and instead found relief." Another client described their 'Place of Joy' as a rainy afternoon on a wide porch, the soft patter of water on the roof, and a deep chair that held him in warmth and safety. Someone else found her joy on a quiet beach, the steady rhythm of waves matching her breath. Yet another rested beneath tall pines, on a bed of fragrant needles, listening to the babble of a nearby brook.

As therapy progresses, many clients refine or change their 'Place of Joy' finding new scenes that mirror their healing. They often expect past lives to reveal trauma. Yet just as often, they encounter peace. One elderly man reflected, "I was expecting troubled lives and instead I found this ordinary, uncomplicated time. I was aware and relieved by the absence of pain and anxiety, and I enjoyed the presence of a simple, calm feeling of comfort.

The sun was shining on me, and I basked in its warmth and the encompassing safety of my father's love. It was as though there never needed to be any intensity, no peaks and valleys. There were no more questions, it all just was." That moment became his permanent 'Place of Joy.'

This method can be used not only for past life exploration but also for trauma recovery. We employ it with individuals facing PTSD, chronic pain, grief, chronic illness, loss, and/or severe mental health crises. We also use it with families navigating end-of-life care. Frequently, we work with other practitioners in a continuum of collaborative care depending on the diagnosis and needs of the clients. In many instances, we find that this method provides an effective bridge between the spirituality of traditional healing and modern medical science.

Families often choose to participate together. Husbands and wives, parents and children, grandparents, uncles and aunts, or other family members of choice may share the experience. Together they discover that it strengthens their connection and resilience. When challenges arise later, they can recall their sanctuary, reminding one another of calm, serenity, and love. This shared practice reinforces their awareness of endurance and resilience across generations, the continuity of spirit that transcends time and circumstance.

Method

Before beginning hypnotherapy, each client and family member is invited to share their life story. Together, we construct a genogram, mapping the intergenerational patterns of family history (McGoldrick et al., 2020). The genogram is the family professional's way of portraying the family tree. We also review prior medical and therapeutic experiences, medications, and relevant health concerns. This context helps us recognize recurring dynamics, unfinished emotional business, and significant figures who may reappear across lifetimes. A spouse in this life may once have been a parent, child, or trusted companion; a family friend may resurface as a healer or guide. These repeating relationships often illuminate the deeper lessons of love, forgiveness, and growth.

For families unsure of their ancestry, we use metaphor: "*What might have happened? Where did your people come from? What trials did they overcome: war, famine, displacement?*" The realization that one's lineage has survived countless challenges helps clients reconnect with their inherent resilience.

Once we have a clear picture, we ask what the client wishes to achieve. Often, there is a symptom or recurring struggle that has resisted previous interventions. Success depends on trust – on creating a safe space where the client feels free to share even their most private thoughts. We employ a variety of hypnotic induction techniques, allowing each person to move at their own pace.

Guided Imagery: The client envisions a place of beauty and security, a beach, a forest, a quiet room, or even a snowy mountainside. Some hypnotherapists use a rapid induction with a pendulum or a simple count of three, often accompanied by a finger snap or gentle tap on the forehead. We prefer to have the client fully relaxed and then use guided imagery for a gradual induction.

- Many of our clients are either anxious or believe firmly that they can never be hypnotized. We have found that using a progressive relaxation exercise (Jacobson, 1938; McGuigan & Lehrer, 2021) before the induction can help calm their anxiety. For those who struggle to relax, we work with them on specialized breathing techniques, controlled breathing, synchronized inhalations, or alternate nostril breathing to ease the transition into a hypnotic state.
- Each client chooses their own path into the process: descending steps, walking a garden path, floating on calm waters, slowly descending into the ocean, or entering through a symbolic door or gate. Whenever anxiety arises, we guide them back to their 'Place of Joy' before continuing.

Throughout each session, we keep careful notes and encourage the client to do the same. Insights and vivid recollections often continue between sessions, gradually filling in the story. These reflections are essential, as growth comes not from a completed narrative but from the unfolding awareness itself. The client remains the expert on their own journey and their memories. Their journals provide the guide.

During debriefing, we review both sets of notes, theirs and ours, to clarify goals for the next session. This reflection is where much of the true healing occurs, when the client and family integrate emotional release, forgiveness, and understanding.

There are times during the hypnotherapy session when clients and families are likely to experience heightened anxiety. For example, when a client approaches the moment of death in a past life, fear sometimes arises and both client and family may become very upset. A brief return to the 'Place of Joy' restores courage and calm. At other times, we help them gently float out of their body to observe the transition without distress. In this safe space, they may meet significant figures from that lifetime, offer forgiveness, and understand the purpose of this shared experience. Here, there is no judgment, no regret, only clarity, compassion, and the quiet knowledge of purpose. It is a realm of renewal, where the soul gathers wisdom and shapes the blueprint for lives yet to come.

Many clients reconnect with companions from other incarnations; souls who have walked beside them time and again. They clarify misunderstandings, release lingering pain, and recognize the deeper threads weaving their relationships together across time. Past life discoveries are often rich and surprising. Even traumatic memories can provide understanding about persistent emotional or physical patterns. Healing also often takes place in the space between lives – a realm of peace and wisdom where guides and loved ones gather, reviewing what has been learned and preparing for what is to come.

The worlds to which our clients travel may be humble or grand, radiant or shadowed. It is our privilege to accompany them, when invited, to witness their light, their grief, and their discoveries. At times, we sense the brightness of a desert sun, the cool hush of a forest, or the ache of loss. Always, we remain humble and grateful for the trust bestowed upon us. We take care never to impose our own impressions. This is their journey, their truth. We hold no secrets from them; the insight belongs to the traveler.

Clients often ask, "*What is real?*" We invite them to decide for themselves. Whether they view their experiences as literal reincarnation, as manifestations of the collective unconscious (Jung, 1991), or as symbolic metaphor, the healing is equally real. As Steve Burgess (2025) reminds us, "Often, as a result of this, we gain a greater awareness of our present life too. The traumas in the past that are holding us back are in 3 areas: this present lifetime; past lives; our ancestor's lives." (para. 2.)[2]

Our 50-plus years of work with individuals and families using Past Life Regression Hypnotherapy and the 'Place of Joy' method continues to affirm our faith in the human spirit. Time and again, we witness human resilience and the capacity for love, peace, and transformation. This work reminds us that no matter how far back or forward we travel, the essence we discover is always the same – love and joy.

Notes

1 Gale, G. (2025, December). Personal communication. Dr. Gale calls this light state of hypnosis, "relational meditation."

2 Burgess (2025), Woolger (1988), Krasner (1997).

References

Altenburger, L. E., Schoppe-Sullivan, S. J., Lang, S. N., Bower, D. J., & Kamp Dush, C. M. (2014). Associations between prenatal coparenting behavior and observed coparenting behavior at 9-months postpartum. *Journal of Family Psychology*, 28(4), 495–504.

American Psychiatric Association. (2006). *American Psychiatric Association practice guidelines for the treatment of psychiatric disorders: Compendium 2006*. American Psychiatric Association.

American Psychiatric Association. (2013). *Diagnostic and statistical manual of mental disorders* (5th ed.). American Psychiatric Association.

American Psychiatric Association. (2022). *Diagnostic and statistical manual of mental disorders* (5th ed., text rev.). American Psychiatric Publishing.

Anastasiadou, D., Medina-Pradas, C., Sepulveda, A. R., & Treasure, J. (2014). A systematic review of family caregiving in eating disorders. *Eating Behaviors*, 15, 464–477.

Beck, A. T. (1979). *Cognitive therapy of depression*. Guilford Press.

Bender, M. L. (1997). *The Nilo-Saharan languages: A comparative essay*. Rüdiger Köppe Verlag.

Benoit, D. (2004). Infant–parent attachment: Definition, types, antecedents, measurement and outcome. *Paediatrics & Child Health*, 9(8), 541–545.

Boss, P. (2006). *Loss, trauma, and resilience: Therapeutic work with ambiguous loss*. W. W. Norton & Company.

Boszormenyi-Nagy, I., & Spark, G. M. (1973). *Invisible loyalties: Reciprocity in intergenerational family therapy*. Harper & Row.

Burgess, S. (2020). *The power of past life regression*. 6th Books.

Burgess, S. (2025). *The adventures of a hypnotherapist: "Was I Under?"*. O-Books.

Clare, G. (2025). *5 steps to talk about intergenerational trauma with your family*. Good Therapy.

Couturier, J., Kimber, M., & Szatmari, P. (2013). Efficacy of family-based treatment for adolescents with eating disorders: A systematic review and meta-analysis. *International Journal of Eating Disorders*, 46(1), 3–11.

Donald, G. M. Jr. (2011a, June 27). Article in The New York Times.

Donald, P. R. (2011b). Rinderpest: The second animal disease to be eradicated. *South African Medical Journal*, 101(2), 65–66.

Ehret, C. (2001). *A historical–comparative reconstruction of Nilo-Saharan*. Rüdiger Köppe Verlag.

Engel, G. L. (1977). The need for a new medical model: A challenge for biomedicine. *Science*, 196(4286), 129–136.

Espie, J., & Eisler, I. (2015). Focus on family therapy in anorexia nervosa: Evidence and challenges. *International Journal of Child and Adolescent Health*, 8(1), 1–12.

Falicov, C. J. (2012). Immigrant family processes: A multidimensional framework (MECA). In F. Walsh (Ed.), *Normal family processes* (pp. 297–323). Guilford Press.

Felitti, V. J., Anda, R. F., Nordenberg, D., Williamson, D. F., Spitz, A. M., Edwards, V., Koss, M. P., & Marks, J. S. (1998). Relationship of childhood abuse and household dysfunction to many of the leading causes of death in adults: The Adverse Childhood Experiences (ACE) Study. *American Journal of Preventive Medicine*, 14(4), 245–258.

Fisher, C. A., Skocic, S., Rutherford, K. A., & Hetrick, S. E. (2018). Family therapy approaches for anorexia nervosa. *Cochrane Database of Systematic Reviews*, 2018(10), CD004780.

Fitzpatrick, K. K., Moye, A., Hoste, R., Lock, J., & Le Grange, D. (2010). Adolescent-focused therapy for adolescents with anorexia nervosa. *Journal of Contemporary Psychotherapy*, 40(1), 31–39.

Framo, J. L. (1992). *Family-of-origin therapy: An intergenerational approach*. Brunner/Mazel.

Franco, F. (2023). Intergenerational transmission of trauma. *Journal of Health Service Psychology*, 49, 185–190.

Garrett, J., & Landau, J. (2007). Family Motivation to Change: A major factor in engaging alcoholics in treatment. *Alcoholism Treatment Quarterly*, 25(1/2), 65–83.

Godart, N. T., Berthoz, S., Curt, F., Perdereau, F., Rein, Z., Wallier, J., Huas, C., & Falissard, B. (2012). A randomized controlled trial of adjunctive family therapy and treatment as usual following inpatient treatment for anorexia nervosa adolescents. *PLOS ONE*, 7(6), e3812.

Hahlweg, K., & Baucom, D. H. (2023). Family therapy for persons with schizophrenia: Neglected yet important. *European Archives of Psychiatry and Clinical Neuroscience*, 273(4), 819–824.

Haley, J. (1976). *Problem-solving therapy*. Jossey-Bass.

Hay, P., Chinn, D., Forbes, D., Madden, S., Newton, R., Sugenor, L., Touyz, S., & Ward, W. (2014). Royal Australian and New Zealand College of psychiatrists clinical practice guidelines for the treatment of eating disorders. *Australian & New Zealand Journal of Psychiatry*, 48(11), 977–1008.

Herman, J. L. (2015). *Trauma and recovery: The aftermath of violence—from domestic abuse to political terror*. Basic Books.

Herpertz-Dahlmann, B., Schwarte, R., Krei, M., Egberts, K., Warnke, A., Wewetzer, C., Pfeiffer, E., Fleischhaker, C., Scherag, A., & Hebebrand, J. (2015). Day-patient treatment after short inpatient care versus continued inpatient treatment in adolescents with anorexia nervosa (ANDI): A multicentre, randomised, open-label, non-inferiority trial. *The Lancet*, 385(9976), 551–559.

Jacobson, E. (1938). *Progressive relaxation*. University of Chicago Press.

Jones, M. G., Rice, S. M., & Cotton, S. M. (2019). Incorporating animal-assisted therapy in mental health treatments for adolescents: A systematic review of canine assisted psychotherapy. *PLOS ONE*, 14(1), e0210761.

Jung, C. G. (1991). *The archetypes and the collective unconscious* (R. F. C. Hull Trans.; 2nd ed.). Routledge UK.

Kamioka, H., Okada, S., Tsutani, K., Park, H., Okuizumi, H., Handa, S., Oshio, T., Park, S.-J., Kitayuguchi, J., Abe, T., Honda, T., & Mutoh, Y. (2014). Effectiveness of animal-assisted therapy: A systematic review of randomized controlled trials. *Complementary Therapies in Medicine*, 22(2), 371–390.

Krasner, A. M. (1997). *The wizard within: The Krasner method of clinical hypnotherapy*. American Board of Hypnotherapy Press.

Landau, J. (1982). Therapy with families in cultural transition. In M. McGoldrick, J. K. Pearce, & J. Giordano (Eds.), *Ethnicity and family therapy* (pp. 552–572). Guilford Press. (Translated & reprinted 1983 in Reseaux-Systèmes-Agencements.)

Landau, J., & Stanton, M.D. (1983). Therapeutic intervention: Families with adolescent substance abusers. *Focus on Alcohol and Drug Issues*, 6(3), 2–3.

Landau, J. L. (2018). Transitional family therapy. In J. Lebow, A. Chambers, & D. Breunlin (Eds.), *Encyclopedia of couple and family therapy*. Springer.

Landau-Stanton, J. (1985). Adolescents, families, and cultural transition: A treatment model. In M.P. Mirkin & S.L. Koman (Eds.), *Handbook of adolescents and family therapy* (pp. 363–381). Gardner Press.

Le Grange, D., & Eisler, I. (2009). Family interventions in adolescent anorexia nervosa. *Child and Adolescent Psychiatric Clinics of North America*, 18(1), 159–173.

Le Grange, D., Lock, J., Loeb, K., & Nicholls, D. (2010). Academy for Eating Disorders position paper: The role of the family in eating disorders. *International Journal of Eating Disorders*, 43(1), 1–5.

Lebow, J., Chambers, A., & Breunlin, D. (Eds.). (2018). *Encyclopedia of couple and family therapy*. Springer.

Leong, F. T. L., Callahan, J. L., Zimmerman, J., Constantino, M. J., & Eubanks, C. F. (Eds.). (2023). *APA handbook of psychotherapy* (Vols. 1–2). American Psychological Association.

Lock, J. (2011). Evaluation of family treatment models for eating disorders. *Current Opinion in Psychiatry*, 24, 274–279.

Lock, J. (2015). An update on evidence-based psychosocial treatments for eating disorders in children and adolescents. *Journal of Clinical Child & Adolescent Psychology*, 44(5), 707–721.

Lyke, J., & Matsen, J. (2013). Family functioning and eating disorders: A comparison of clinical and nonclinical families. *Eating Disorders*, 21(1), 1–13.

Martin, A. R. (1942). *Researches in reincarnation and beyond*. Psychic Research Company.

Maujean, A., Pepping, C. A., & Kendall, E. (2015). A systematic review of randomized controlled trials of animal-assisted therapy on psychosocial outcomes. *Anthrozoös*, 28(1), 23–36.

Mayo Clinic. (2022, December 13).

McGoldrick, M., Gerson, R., & Petry, S. (2020). *Genograms: Assessment and treatment*. W. W. Norton & Company.

McGuigan, F. J., & Lehrer, P. M. (2021). Progressive relaxation: Origins, principles, and clinical applications. In P. M. Lehrer & R. L. Woolfolk (Eds.), *Principles and practice of stress management* (4th ed., pp. 151–192). The Guilford Press.

Miklowitz, D. J. (2007). The role of the family in the course of bipolar illness. *American Journal of Family Therapy*, 35(5), 381–401.

Minuchin, S, & Fishman, H. C. (1981). *Family therapy techniques*. Harvard University Press.

Montalvo, B. (1996). Review of La esclavitud de las dietas: Guia para reconocer y encarar un trastorno alimentario, by C. R. Herscovici. *Families, Systems, & Health*, 14(3), 397–398.

Murray, S. B., & Le Grange, D. (2014). Family therapy for adolescent eating disorders: An update. *Current Opinion in Psychiatry*, 27(6), 455–460.

National Institute for Health and Care Excellence. (2004). *Eating disorders: Core interventions in the treatment and management of anorexia nervosa, bulimia nervosa and related eating disorders (Clinical guideline CG9)*. NICE.

Otis, J. D., Keller, A. E., & Chevalier, L. (2021). Cognitive behavioral therapy for chronic pain. In A. Wenzel (Ed.), *Handbook of cognitive behavioral therapy: Applications* (pp. 423–451). American Psychological Association

Plowman, J. (1996). Past life memories and present day problems. *European Journal of Clinical Hypnosis*, 3(2), 36–39.

Pohl, M. (2012). *A day without pain* (Rev. ed.). Central Recovery Press.

Pohl, M., & Ketcham, K. (2015). *The pain antidote*. Da Capo Lifelong Books.

Porges, S. W. (2011). *The polyvagal theory: Neurophysiological foundations of emotions, attachment, communication, and self-regulation*. W. W. Norton & Company.

Rikani, A. A., Choudhry, Z., Choudhry, A. M., Ikram, H., Asghar, M. W., Kajal, D., Waheed, A., & Mobassarah, N. J. (2013). A critique of the literature on aetiology of eating disorders. *Annals of Neurosciences*, 20(4), 157–161.

Roberts, J. (1972). *Seth speaks: The eternal validity of the soul*. Prentice-Hall.

Rosenthal, M. (2021). Intergenerational trauma: An embodied experience. *International Body Psychotherapy Journal*, 20(2), 45–57.

Roy, R., de la Vega, R., Jensen, M. P., & Miró, J. (2020). Neurofeedback for pain management: A systematic review. *Frontiers in Neuroscience*, 14, 671.

Schwartz, R. C. (1995). *Internal family systems therapy*. Guilford Press.

Schwartz, S. J., Unger, J. B., Zamboanga, B. L., & Szapocznik, J. (2010). Rethinking the concept of acculturation: Implications for theory and research. *American Psychologist*, 65(4), 237–251.

Seaburn, D., Landau-Stanton, J., and Horwitz, S. (1995). Core techniques in family therapy. In R. H. Mikesell, D. Lusterman, & S. H. McDaniel (Eds.), *Integrating family therapy: Handbook of family psychology and systems theory* (pp. 5–26). American Psychological Association.

Shapiro, F. (2018). *Eye movement desensitization and reprocessing (EMDR) therapy: Basic principles, protocols, and procedures* (3rd ed.). Guilford Press.

Sim, L. A., Homme, J. H., Lteif, A. N., Vande Voort, J. L., Schak, K. M., & Ellingson, J. (2009). Family functioning and maternal distress in adolescent girls with anorexia nervosa. *International Journal of Eating Disorders*, 42(6), 531–539.

Sluzki, C. (1969). Migration and family conflict. *Family Process*, 18(4), 379–390.

Sluzki, C. E. (2008). Migration and the disruption of the social network. In M. McGoldrick & K. V. Hardy (Eds.), *Re-visioning family therapy* (pp. 39–47). Guilford Press.

Sommers-Flanagan, J., & Sommers-Flanagan, R. (2018). *Counseling and psychotherapy theories in context and practice* (3rd ed.). John Wiley & Sons.

Stanton, M. D., & Todd, T. C. (Eds.). (1982). *Family therapy of drug abuse and addiction*. Guilford Press.

Sullivan, A. E., Judd, C. M., Axelson, D. A., & Miklowitz, D. J. (2012). Family functioning and the course of adolescent bipolar disorder. *Behavior Therapy*, 43(4), 837–847.

Tomlinson, A. (2006). Beyond past lives and into the soul memories between lives: Applications of hypnosis. *European Journal of Clinical Hypnosis*, 7(2), 18–25.

Van der Kolk, B. A. (2014). *The body keeps the score: Brain, mind, and body in the healing of trauma*. Viking.

Walsh, F., & McGoldrick, M. (Eds.). (1991). *Living beyond loss: Death in the family*. W. W. Norton & Company.

Weigensberg, M. J., Morecki, S., Weiss, L., Fuks, Z., & Slavin, S. (1984). Radiation-induced malignancies following childhood thymus irradiation. *Cancer*, 54(5), 1000–1005.

Weiss, B. L. (1988). *Many lives, many masters*. Simon & Schuster.

Weiss, B. L. (1996). *Only love is real: A story of soul mates reunited*. Warner Books.

Woolger, R. J. (1988). *Other lives, other selves: A Jungian psychotherapist discovers past lives*. Random House.

Index

For Product Safety Concerns and Information please contact our EU representative GPSR@taylorandfrancis.com
Taylor & Francis Verlag GmbH, Kaufingerstraße 24, 80331 München, Germany

www.ingramcontent.com/pod-product-compliance
Ingram Content Group UK Ltd.
Pitfield, Milton Keynes, MK11 3LW, UK
UKHW022121190926
475702UK00013B/1570

9781041065906